William Ayers : *about Becoming a Teacher*

sj Miller : *about Gender Identity Justice in Schools and Communities*

about
BECOMING A TEACHER

WILLIAM AYERS

TEACHERS COLLEGE PRESS

TEACHERS COLLEGE | COLUMBIA UNIVERSITY
NEW YORK AND LONDON

Published by Teachers College Press, 1234 Amsterdam Avenue, New York, NY 10027

Library of Congress Cataloging-in-Publication Data

Names: Ayers, William, 1944- author.
Title: about becoming a teacher / William Ayers.
Description: New York, NY : Teachers College Press, [2019] | Series: School : questions |
Identifiers: LCCN 2018058243 (print) | LCCN 2019002469 (ebook) | ISBN 9780807777886 (ebook) | ISBN 9780807761496 (pbk. : alk. paper)
Subjects: LCSH: Teaching—Vocational guidance. | Education—Study and teaching.
Classification: LCC LB1775 (ebook) | LCC LB1775 .A94 2019 (print) | DDC 371.10023—dc23
LC record available at https://lccn.loc.gov/2018058243

ISBN 978-0-8077-6149-6 (paper)
ISBN 978-0-8077-6167-0 (hardcover)
ISBN 978-0-8077-7788-6 (ebook)

Printed on acid-free paper
Manufactured in the United States of America

*For **Nala Marie**,*
a mighty miracle who'll be in 1st grade in the year 2022

Contents

Singing in Dark Times

A Series Introduction

> In the dark times, will there also be singing?
> Yes, there will be singing.
> About the dark times.

—Bertolt Brecht, "Motto"

As neoliberalism persists and fascism seems to lurk close by, and as the public is being eroded and steadily eclipsed, those who believe in freedom and justice must take responsibility to reimagine, revitalize, and re-create the public square, a broader public presence, and a wider range of participatory public spaces.

School : Questions is one modest attempt to step up to that challenge, and to fulfill what we take to be our moral and political responsibility to deepen a common conversation focused on public education and this political moment.

The school struggles of the past several decades have too often masked a fundamental underlying disagreement and question: Is public education a product to be sold in the marketplace like a pair of shoes or a laptop, or is it a fundamental human right and a community responsibility? We take the human rights position, and point to Article 26 of the Universal Declaration of Human Rights (1948), which reads in part, "Everyone has the right to education [which] . . . shall be directed to the full development of the human personality and to the strengthening of respect for human rights and fundamental freedoms."

In the current sweep of public school reform it may seem that those who promote schooling as a market-based product—the privatizers and the marketeers—have won the day, hold all the cards, and wield all the power, but that's simply not the case. True, they have a lot of money and resources, foundation endorsements, an amen chorus from the for-profit media and the chattering class, and the acquiescence of major players in the two dominant political parties. That's a lot, and it can seem overwhelming, but look more closely at what the corporate reformers are missing, even after decades of dangling the carrots and wielding the big sticks: They have not won over a majority of teachers and students or parents and community members, and they have not quelled the opposition or the resistance to their "reform" initiatives, which is only growing. Most important, they have not developed a convincing moral argument for the dismantling of well-resourced, excellent public schools that are accessible to every child regardless of condition, location, or background.

School : Questions is a series of concise, pointed texts grounded in an embrace of the belief that an excellent public school experience is the right of every child and the responsibility of every community. Each book is designed as a sharp intervention—relevant and hard-hitting—in one or another of the most urgent and necessary discussions concerning the problems and possibilities with public schools today. Each of these compact texts can be deployed as a catalyst in the urgent work of reframing the debates swirling around (and mystifying or clouding) public educational policy and practice today. Each is small by design, something to slip comfortably into your backpack next to the water and the vitamin C, and something to read on the train or the bus on your way to class, a school board meeting, a city council hearing, or a public demonstration.

While we cannot choose our time nor our moment in the light, we must choose who to be in face of these facts. In these volatile and desperate times we choose the cause of humanity—the ongoing struggles for more peace, more recognition, more equity, more access, more fairness.

—William Ayers, Chicago, Illinois, January 2019

CHAPTER : ONE

Should I Become a Teacher?

You think you want to teach?

Terrific! Go for it!

I'm a passionate advocate for teachers and a fiery partisan of good teaching, and so my instinct is to enthusiastically applaud your choice. Onward and upward!

But let's not get ahead of ourselves. Before we get too high on the idea or too caught up in wild celebration, and before we head too far down that particular path, let's consider if teaching is right for you, and, on the other side, whether you have the dispositions of mind and the potential skills to become an outstanding classroom teacher—or, not to be too lofty about it, to become a good and successful teacher. We'll look at some first issues, a few of the basics, and some more fundamental matters, like, What is teaching anyway? What does it look like at its best? Who is this person we call "teacher"?

But let's first consider a prior question, quick and simple: Has anyone ever told you NOT to teach? Your friends, perhaps, or your partner? Your parents, or your brother or sister? Maybe a favorite teacher, someone who inspired you and then, when you expressed a desire to follow in those exciting footsteps, discouraged you, enumerating in detail the challenges one faces in a life of teaching, and urging you to find another calling? "Oh, Lord, whatever you do, don't become a teacher!" That must have been disheartening.

These are all people who care about you—some of them even love you—so why are you ignoring their advice? It isn't easy, I know, because for many years the "Don't Teach" chorus followed me like a swarm of flies on a hot summer's day, annoyingly buzzing in my ears from morning till night.

Ignoring them was impossible, and swatting them away was never entirely successful.

Being married to a lawyer for many years, I often find myself at lawyer parties. In all the years I taught elementary, middle school, and early childhood education, my interactions over wine and cheese became completely predictable: Lawyer: What do you do? Me: I teach kindergarten (or in other years, I teach in the Juvenile Detention Center, or, I teach middle school). Lawyer (a pitying, patronizing look crossing his face): That must be *interesting*. At which point he rushes off to talk with someone he finds really interesting.

Of course, many of us who teach or who are headed toward teaching have been counseled at some point or another to consider a dramatic change of direction, to come to our senses and to search out an alternative profession or career. We're advised that we won't get rich if we choose a life in teaching, and of course that's true. Your likely response to that unhelpful comment was, "Duh!," but if you've been living under a rock, and you've dreamed that teaching will magically put you on the road to riches, we should stop right here so that I can explain. But my guess is that it never even crossed your mind, and that when you thought about being a teacher as opposed to a variety of other occupations you might have pursued, you never pictured yourself amassing a fortune and rolling around the classroom in barrels of cash—the prospect of easy money likely played no part at all in your calculation or your decision.

We've also all been cautioned regularly by friends and family that teaching won't earn us the respect that we deserve for the real work that we do day in and day out, and that's true as well. While salary is only a crude measure of social regard and community esteem, it's probably worth noting that I've worked over many years as a stevedore, a merchant marine, and a truck driver as well as a schoolteacher, and in each of those other jobs I earned more money than I ever made teaching, with the added advantage that at the end of my shift, with my labor bought and paid for, I left work behind without a backward glance—and that stands in sharp contrast to the all-consuming, 24/7 nature of teaching, where every challenge, missed opportunity, or future plan can haunt you or at least occupy your mind for days and weeks at a time. U.S. teachers earn only 77% on average of what other college graduates make, and that strikes many of us as shameful. But in some ways even more egregious is to note the ways that teachers have become perennial punching bags for grandstanding politicians and empty talking heads who use us as convenient targets for every social ill we collectively face. Teachers, we're told, are all unmotivated placeholders grown lazy in the sinecure of government employment, our incompetence papered over by self-interested, special-interest unions. We make too much money for too little work, we're told, blow holes in city and state budgets, are lazy and incompetent, and are responsible for failing to curb drug and alcohol abuse, teen pregnancy, suicide, and the rising economy of China, just for starters.

These are troubling times for teachers, to be sure, in part because those powerful and noisy forces parading under the banner of "reform" have their sights set on further disempowering and de-skilling teachers (teacher-proof curriculum is one fraudulent example, virtual and online "schools" are others), reducing them to clerks and auditors rather than the relationship-builders and agents of enlightenment, liberation, and transformation that they aspire (and work hard every day) to be. These "reformers" conceive of education as a product to be bought and sold in the marketplace, promote privatizing one aspect after another of a school's vital functions, and frame teachers as assembly-line workers pouring knowledge into the upturned heads of passive students as they bump along the K–12 conveyor belt called school. The deeper design of the "reformers" has become crystal clear: They are determined to devour public education altogether.

There's a more hopeful and helpful truth within reach: Children and youth know who cares for them, who values them, who challenges and nourishes them and takes their side. Students value good teachers, and parents do too. That's your real audience, and those are your lifelong partners in learning .

: : :

Perhaps unintentionally, perhaps not, this crop of "reformers" brings to mind an indelible image of teaching taken from the dawn of the Industrial Revolution. While the revolutionary Karl Marx (1818–1883) labored away in the library studying economics, history, and philosophy, building his germinal theory of dialectical materialism, his renowned contemporary, the brilliant writer Charles Dickens (1812–1870; *A Christmas Carol, A Tale of Two Cities*), threw in his lot as well with the working and lower classes against the excesses and raw predations of industrial capitalism, with its accompanying philosophy of utilitarianism and its single-minded fascination with averages and statistical analysis at the expense of the sparkling reality of real human beings living their complicated lives. I have a picture in my mind of Marx and Dickens sitting across from one another in a vast reading room at the British Museum, each completely engrossed in the work and failing to notice the other, each casting propulsive words on the page meant to plant seeds of dissent and herald fundamental change.

Dickens's tenth novel, *Hard Times,* opens with a memorable (if chilling) exchange about Fact versus Fancy as the basis of a sound education. I hear all kinds of contemporary echoes in this venerable description of life in classrooms, which is why I return to it again and again in these difficult times for public education and for teachers. See if you hear the echoes as well.

The aptly named Mr. Gradgrind, the owner of a school in an industrial city called Coketown, lectures his hired schoolmaster, Mr. M'Choakumchild, on the finer points of curriculum and instruction:

"Now, what I want is, Facts. Teach these boys and girls nothing but Facts. Facts alone are wanted in life. Plant nothing else, and root out everything else. You can only form the minds of reasoning animals upon Facts; nothing else will ever be of any service to them. This is the principle on which I bring up my own children, and this is the principle on which I bring up these children. Stick to Facts, Sir!"

The two men looked out at the students, and saw only the upturned heads of empty . . . "vessels then and there arranged in order, ready to have imperial gallons of facts poured into them until they were full to the brim."

To deepen and illustrate his argument, Gradgrind interrogates a child he refers to as "girl number twenty," and, discovering that her father is a horseman, asks her to define a horse. When she stumbles Gradgrind pounces: "Girl number twenty unable to define a horse. . . . Girl number twenty possessed of no facts, in reference to one of the commonest of animals!" He turns to a boy who obediently stands and recites: "Quadruped. Graminivorous. Forty teeth, namely twenty-four grinders, four eye-teeth, and twelve incisive. . . ." And on and on, numbers and norms, at the end of which Gradgrind nods approvingly and notes, "Now girl number twenty, you know what a horse is."

Girl number twenty knows plenty about horses, of course, and a number of other things as well. She's a three-dimensional person with agency and a mind and a spirit, a heart and a body, experiences and hopes and dreams just like every other human being. She has compassion for others and a fine sense of aesthetics, and she has a broad imagination, which she calls her "Fancy," all qualities Gradgrind finds irrelevant if not abhorrent.

In these opening chapters (one appropriately called "The Murder of Innocents"), Dickens evokes the broad outlines of autocratic classrooms in all times and places. It's a kind of meditation on the power of these men of facts-without-feeling to crush or twist natural human dispositions and sympathies.

I don't think any of us should want to go back there.

The scene underlines the point that the powerful in any society build the schools that will serve their interests: Monarchies promote an education of fealty first and foremost; theocracies create schools of orthodoxy and obedience. Schools no matter where or when are always mirror and window into whatever larger social order creates and sustains them, and we can, therefore, easily imagine what kind of society those "imperial gallons of facts" are meant to sustain and reproduce. What is a bit surprising, however, is to find a portrait of schooling in Victorian England that so eerily evokes a modern American classroom—how strange. Or maybe not—perhaps Dickens's Victorian classrooms, with their imperious reasoning and brute, despotic logic, are familiar to us a century and a half later precisely because the needs of global finance capital today are quite similar: A disciplined working class divided into hard hierarchies of winners and losers; a large segment destined for the prisons and the unemployment lines; a few trained as managers and disciplinarians; and 1% destined to reap the profits of a predatory, invasive system.

: : :

As you proceed and move forward toward teaching, bear in mind that this is a particularly unstable time for the profession, and, as noted, becoming a teacher won't secure you a spot on the Fortune 500 list of the indecently rich, nor will it elevate your status to celebrity-toast-of-the-town territory. But probably that's OK because most of you never thought that being a teacher would do any of those things for you anyway—teaching was never about fame and fortune, money or social rank. Let's forget about it and move on.

There's one more potential obstacle I'd like you to consider before we take a closer look at those first, fundamental questions concerning the nature and the reality of teaching: the common representations of teachers and teaching in mass culture and major media. This is a problem because the most familiar images of teachers are untrustworthy at best, and

sometimes fraudulent to the point of absurdity, but they flood our consciousness nonetheless, and they seem to carry a magic power that can
shape our perceptions of what to expect in the work ahead—even when our
lived experiences directly contradict those dominant images.

The enduring portrayal of teachers in popular films—from *Blackboard
Jungle* to *Stand and Deliver, Dangerous Minds, Freedom Writers*, and beyond—is the solitary teacher-hero fighting valiantly to save the good juvenile delinquents from the sewers of their circumstances. Terrible families,
rotten neighborhoods, deplorable peers, overburdened schools, and indifferent teachers—the hero-teacher is resisted at every turn and defied from
every direction, and yet she or he perseveres and wins. Teaching as salva-
tion and as drama.

And it's true: Teaching is drama, but it's so much more. It's also hard
daily work that draws on a person's deepest intelligences as well as unfath-
omable reserves of energy, a daily grind that is excruciatingly complex,
filled with discovery and surprise, improvisation and invention, creativity
and imagination, joy and also frustration! You will experience profound
challenges and periods of loneliness; you will feel discouraged some of the
time and over your head much of the time, and this is when you will have
to dig deep within yourself—and reach outside yourself to fellow teachers,
parents, and students—in order to regroup and rise up stronger.

> If you're going to get into the classroom with your head screwed on straight and your mind somewhat intact, beware of—and resist!—the received wisdom, clichés, and popular images of teachers teaching.

I'll address strategies for coping and sur-
viving further on, but note that none of the
common images of teachers teaching wres-
tles with the real daily difficulties or challenges teachers face, nor pays much attention
to the art of teaching nor to the science of it;
none is wide enough nor deep enough, none
vital enough to capture the trembling reality
of actual teaching. None goes directly to the
heart of the experience—to the intellectual demand, to the ethical purpose
or the moral meaning, to the larger spirit that can animate each classroom
as well as the whole enterprise. What's mostly missing, even in seemingly
benign depictions, is a sense of the soul of teaching. It is this territory—
teaching as a relentlessly moral endeavor, teaching as ethical action, messy,
grand, and tangled—that cries out urgently to be explored. If you're going
to get into the classroom with your head screwed on straight and your mind
somewhat intact, beware of—and resist!—the received wisdom, clichés,

and popular images of teachers teaching, as well as the nasty and hazardous stereotypes about particular parents or neighborhoods or kids.

Resist as well most of the scholarly literature in which teachers are dissected and measured, talked about but rarely listened to, and their performances set against student outcomes—"scientized" teaching and teachers as data. As the men with the megaphones holler about "data-driven teaching," stay true to a different ideal: Teaching that is *student-driven* while data-informed. You can be knowledgeable about research and sophisticated about facts and figures without ever falling into data's arid and dreary thrall.

: : :

So these are a few items on my list of things to avoid or resist, but let's move from the negative to the positive, from the gloomy to the bright and hopeful. Let's talk about the heart and soul of teaching, the vivid expectations you have for yourself and others, the wildest dreams and passionate aspirations that *call* you to teach. What ideal of teaching do you aspire to? What do you think teaching should look like in a free and democratic society? And how do we understand the hopes and practices of this person we call "teacher"?

We begin by thinking clearly about what teaching is at its best, what teaching can be or might still become, and what, at its heart, invites us to become teachers. No one goes into teaching saying, "I'm so excited to get into my own classroom where I can sort children into winners and losers," or, "All my life I've dreamt of prepping youth day after day to take the high-stakes standardized tests," or, "I've worked out an amazing classroom management scheme, and I can't wait to see how well I can control and disciple the little bastards." No teacher thinks like that—OK, there may be someone somewhere, but you don't think that way, and I don't either. We come to teaching from a more hopeful and humane place.

What motivates some of us to teach is an affection or even a love for children or youth, or perhaps the positive feelings generated when we're in the adventurous company of the young. For others it's a passionate engagement with the world or some part of the world—music or math, say, African American history or poetry, geometry or geography—that invites us to share that enthusiasm with young people. Still others cherish a deep sense that education can change the direction of history and society, or perhaps, more modestly, change the people who will change our communities in promising ways. We come to teaching hoping to make a difference—in children's lives and in the larger world.

All of this defines teaching as ethical and intellectual work—more than a job, teaching is a calling, a passion, a vocation—in fact, teaching is the vocation of vocations because a teacher's work is to shepherd the vocations of others, to open all kinds of vistas that will allow the young to choose their own vocations and to discover their own life missions in an expanding universe of choices. Clearly teaching requires a thoughtful and caring person at its heart if it's to be done well. And, yes, not to get too grand about it—it's also a job.

> Teaching is the vocation of vocations because a teacher's work is to shepherd the vocations of others.

Are you willing to explore and discover who you are, deeply and comprehensively, and who you might become as a teacher? Do you have the courage to do basic research on yourself, which includes a willingness to recognize your own strengths and failures? Can you acknowledge what you don't know or haven't figured out yet? And are you willing to commit to teaching as a *practice*, an ongoing life project of discovery and surprise about the world, about other people, and, yes, even about yourself?

The intellectual and ethical work of teaching can be hard to see in some places—schools and classrooms that, purposely or not, crush curiosity, impede imagination, and deflate the dreams of youth. These schools and classrooms reward obedience and compliance while punishing creativity and courage, initiative and ingenuity. This is the brutal masquerade called "school" offered to the poor and the traditionally marginalized—to the descendants of formerly enslaved human beings, First Nations peoples, and immigrants from colonized communities. For these mostly Black and Brown and poor kids, the classroom marches under the gauzy banner of enlightenment and democracy, empowerment and progress, even as it operates relentlessly to reproduce and police the hierarchies of winners and losers along predictable lines of race and class. These American schools have inequity and congealed violence baked into their DNA.

Entering our contested classrooms—that space where the eternal conflict between the ideal of teaching and the reality of institutionalized schooling lives—we must think more deeply about our first principles, the tools we carry inside ourselves into teaching every day. The friction is timeless and abiding, and today the contradictions between the ideal and the material are stark: We want to love our students and cherish their learning, and we face an almost pathological obsession from above with student scores on high-stakes standardized tests, the reduction of education to a single metric, the banishment of the arts from classroom life, the near-total disregard for the experiences and collective wisdom of classroom teachers, the systematic dismantling of the public space in favor of private management and private profit, and more.

This is galling for those of us who understand learning to be expansive, dynamic, and idiosyncratic, and who believe that an excellent education is the natural right of every child. And so while we note that we may not have as much control as we'd like concerning the contexts within which we work, we surely have more control than we sometimes recognize or exercise regarding our core values, and choosing how we might live out those values in the dailiness of classroom life. Let's access those values, and let's ask ourselves how we intend to live our teaching lives in a way that doesn't make a mockery of our teaching values.

Teaching in a democracy is geared toward participation and engagement, and it's based, then, on a common faith: Every human being is of infinite and incalculable value, each an intellectual, emotional, physical, spiritual, signifying, and creative universe. Teaching in a free society rests on the twin pillars of enlightenment and liberation, knowledge and human freedom.

> Teaching in a democracy is geared toward participation and engagement, and it's based, then, on a common faith: Every human being is of infinite and incalculable value, each an intellectual, emotional, physical, spiritual, signifying, and creative universe.

Central to an education for citizenship, participation, engagement, and democracy—an education toward freedom—is developing in students and teachers alike the ability to think and speak for themselves. The core curriculum of a liberating education is this: We each have a mind of our own; we are all works in progress swimming toward an uncertain and indeterminate shore; we can each join with others in order to act on our own judgments and in our own freedom; human progress is always the result of thoughtful human activity. We want to assist our students (and we want to join with them, shoulder-to-shoulder, arm-in-arm), as we all escape the telltale stoop of easy compliance.

An emphasis on the needs and interests of each student is co-primary with a faith in the kind of robust public that can be created in classrooms, as well as in the larger society. To be exclusively student-centered, honoring as much as possible each individual student while the needs of the group are ignored or erased, is to develop a kind of fatalistic narcissism; to defer to the group while ignoring the needs of each individual is to destroy any real possibility of freedom. The problem of achieving both individual freedom and collective well-being without sacrificing either one is a problem as old as civilization itself, and while teachers cannot magically resolve this ancient and abiding contradiction, we do have a part to play. We can work diligently and doggedly in our little corner of this one small school to form a community that explicitly lives within and preserves as a creative tension that foundational sense: We are each the one-of-one, and we are, simultaneously, all members of the whole wide community.

Teachers must learn to create classroom spaces of energy and excitement, unlike the sites of coercion and containment that are all too familiar in schools. Everyone is held together in these places we create because they're working along common lines in a communal spirit with shared aims—the difference is motive, spirit, and atmosphere. These are qualities a teacher can uncover and nourish by encouraging and allowing students to move away from being passive recipients of packaged education to choosing themselves as authors, speakers, actors, builders, and makers. In the process we discover that independent thought and conduct have an attraction all their own. The teacher sets the stage, but the actions of students are the heart of learning. This is where classroom teachers discover that teaching is harder than learning in one central aspect: We transform ourselves, becoming students of our students, co-learners and co-teachers. The focus moves away from "teaching" and toward learners learning. We must take a deep breath, step away slightly, and let go. We are learning how to *let learn*.

Are you OK with that?

Then, yes, become a teacher.

CHAPTER : TWO

What Practical Steps Can I Take Right Now to Prepare for a Life in Teaching?

Given where we began in the last chapter, I'm tempted to say, "Save your money!" But, no, I'm not going to say that—too cynical, and conceding too much to the foes of teaching and teachers. Keep your eyes on the prize—the opportunity to work with children and their families, the chance to make a significant positive difference in the lives of the rising generation, and the prospect of becoming an important contributing member of a living community. Teacher. Your own classroom in a school community. That's where you're headed. Keep the faith.

There are, however, several routines or exercises you can undertake on your own—right here, right now—that will help you get ready for the big step into your own classroom that lies just up ahead. You can think of them as teaching calisthenics, workouts that will sharpen your senses while they tone and condition your teaching muscles. These exercises can become part of your daily practice or your weekly regimen alongside (but not as a substitute for) your formal study in education—nothing extraordinary, but simply routine preparation and regular rehearsals.

An obvious exercise is to work with youngsters as a volunteer or coach or paid staff member—after school, day camp, Saturday School, tutoring, play group, club. You will learn a lot about yourself as well as about kids. Also visit as many classrooms as you can, notice everything from seating arrangements to wall displays to room organization, and ask teachers why they made the choices they did. File away what you think is worthwhile for future use.

Another exercise is to think about some of your tentative goals for your future students—for example, I want all the kids in my classes (no matter the subject matter, the age, the level or the grade) to read a broad range of materials for a wide variety of purposes, to read extensively, critically, and well; or, I want all of my students to be able to utilize the whole community (libraries, community centers, businesses, parks, galleries, cinema guilds, theaters, museums, and other cultural institutions) as sites of informal and personalized learning; or, I want to create an environment where my kids can be fearless risk-takers when it comes to learning new things; or, I want my students to engage in civic life; or, I want my class to be a space where everyone becomes a "maker," an author, a composer, a creator. Take a minute and add your own items under the heading: "Some Things I'm Pretty Sure I'll Want All of My Students to Do, to Be, or to Have."

Now, revisit your list and ask yourself this: Do I have in my own daily practice those things I claim to want for all of my students? For example, I might want my students to be risk-takers when it comes to learning—OK, fine. But am I a daring learner myself, someone who stretches and reaches and consistently takes on new challenges? Beyond required courses at college or university, have I taken a class or workshop recently in order to pursue a new interest or develop a new skill? Would that be worthwhile? Maybe you could take a poetry-writing seminar at your local library, guitar lessons at the local Y, a computer graphics or cooking class at the community college, a figure-drawing class at a neighborhood art gallery, bicycle repair instruction at the bike store, a cheese-making workshop at 4-H. Perhaps you could get a designated plot at a community garden, or train to be a docent at the aquarium or the zoo, or take up trampoline or rock climbing or parasailing—the sky's the limit!

Beyond the cheese or the bike or the poetry, though, the point is not to fill up your already overburdened schedule or to engage in meaningless busywork. No. The purpose is to continually practice the art of learning new things, to record the experience in real time, and to remember the feelings, including the awkward cognitive dissonances—dismaying, decentering, embarrassing, and also enlivening and thrilling—that always accompany fresh discoveries. This will help you to connect and to be in sync with your students' emotions, whether they're struggling to master cursive or lurching toward quadratic equations. As an adventuresome learner yourself, your empathy for and understanding of your kids will soar.

You want your students to engage in civic life, fine, but then it's fair to ask if you are actively involved in your community—do you always vote, do you volunteer at the women's shelter, do you feed the homeless, or do you regularly protest injustices? You want your students to utilize the whole community in pursuit of their own growth and learning, OK, so pay attention to how much you regularly access the available resources—do you visit museums and galleries, do you have a season subscription to a local theater? If you want a classroom of "makers," then you ought to be one, too. On and on and on: So perhaps you should add a column next to the items on the "Some Things I'm Pretty Sure I'll Want All of My Students to Do, to Be, or to Have" list, and call it, "Some Specific Ways I'm Developing a Vital Practice in My Own Life Based on Each Item."

Let's return to reading as a final example on this point of animating for yourself those things you most want for youngsters: I assume you want your students to read a range of materials for a variety of purposes—I know I do—and so you need to look in the mirror and ask, Am I reading a wide range of materials for a variety of purposes myself? Do I read for pleasure? Do I go online and check out current events and the breaking news, do I read the newspaper every day, or a couple of magazines every week? Have I read a novel or a history or a biography/autobiography/memoir in the last month? Have I looked at a book of poetry recently, or read a popular book on science in the past half year? No? You can't expect the kids to be bold and constant readers if you yourself are a passive or indifferent one. Get busy! Read more, read better!

Can you name five books that changed your life, or perhaps dramatically altered or expanded your perspective? What do you think you might need to read next to become a better-educated person, a good teacher, an engaged citizen/resident/community member? What literature do you need to dig into

> You can't expect the kids to be bold and constant readers if you yourself are a passive or indifferent one. Get busy! Read more, read better!

more fully in order to broaden your frame of reference or deepen your understanding of your own unique journey, the possibilities up ahead, the choices you'll be called upon to make?

I could give you a list of possible readings available both digitally and in traditional formats—and I'll suggest a few in a moment—but I'm reluctant to offer anything like a definitive catalog because, first, there's no such thing, and, second, then you'd have my list, and not your own, when what you really need is your own list of must-reads. My advice is simple: Read everything. That's right, go to a huge city library, find a seat, and start reading with the impossible goal of reading it all. More realistically, start where you already are, and let one book lead you to other books, one curiosity open to other questions, one interest unlock a treasure chest of related pursuits.

But read deliberately, purposefully—put "reading time" in your calendar or on your schedule, just as you would note the meeting time of a seminar, a dinner with friends, or a doctor's appointment. Make it a 2–3 hour appointment with books—spend one morning a month at an independent bookstore (in Chicago, for example, Seminary Coop/57th Street Books, or Women & Children First, or Volumes, or Unabridged) or just curl up at home for a few hours each week, but you must protect that time diligently: no texting or checking your email, no phone calls or double-booking, just you, your books, a snack, and a cup of coffee or tea. Oh, and at the bookstore locate both the graphic novel section and the children's book area, and hang out there for a while perusing the stacks. You'll find both wonderful reads and interesting fellow readers in each spot.

In among his many drafts of *Leaves of Grass*, quintessential American poet Walt Whitman asserts that reading should never be deployed as a casual distraction:

> Books are call'd for, and supplied, on the assumption that the process of reading is not a half-sleep, but, in highest sense, an exercise, a gymnast's struggle; that the reader is to do something for himself, must be on the alert, must himself or herself construct indeed the poem, argument, history, metaphysical essay—the text furnishing the hints, the clue, the start or frame-work. Not the book needs so much to be the complete thing, but the reader of the book does. That were to make a nation of supple and athletic minds well-train'd, intuitive, used to depend on themselves, and not on a few coteries of writers. (goodreads. com/quotes/8869201-books-are-to-be-call-d-for-and-supplied-on-the)

No reading list can possibly fulfill all of your intellectual aspirations—even in the short run, even over the term of your formal study to become a teacher. I suggest that you begin right now to develop an annotated reading autobiography entitled "My Book of Books: What I'm Reading (and What I'll Need to Read and Why) to Become a More Fully Developed/Educated Person." "My BOB" could be projected 5 years forward, and it should reflect your best thinking on your personal/professional/political/scholarly goals as well as your distinct and idiosyncratic intellectual and ethical journey through school and life. Here are a few that might work for you, or might provoke several other thoughts, but remember, this is my "BOB," not yours—and you really want and need your own Book of Books.

I've found that the most meaningful books on teaching for new teachers are often memoirs, practical stories of folks meeting and overcoming real-life challenges or obstacles in their classrooms as they learn to teach. These texts tend to be nondidactic and holistic, something you can mine again and again for insights and sensible advice grounded in the messy, distinctive world of actual classrooms. Among my favorites are Vivian Gussin Paley, *White Teacher* and *You Can't Say You Can't Play*; Frank McCourt, *Teacher Man*; Greg Michie, *Holler If You Hear Me*; Marvin Hoffman, *Chasing Hellhounds*; Sylvia Ashton-Warner, *Teacher*; and Eliot Wigginton, *Sometimes a Shining Moment*. At the risk of being immodest, I'll add one of mine, a comic book, coauthored with Ryan Alexander-Tanner, *To Teach: The Journey, in Comics*—a happy romp through a young teacher's first year in the classroom.

Other books on education that moved me and taught me new ways of seeing and being include Jay Gillen, *Educating for Insurgency*; Crystal Laura, *Being Bad*; Joel Westheimer, *What Kind of Citizen?*; Noliwe Rooks, *Cutting School*; Mike Rose, *Why School?*; Charles Payne and Carole Strickland, *Teach Freedom*; Elisabeth Soep and Vivian Chavez, *Drop That Knowledge*; Gloria Ladson-Billings, *The Dreamkeepers*; Kevin Kumashiro, *Bad Teacher!*; Jesse Hagopian, *More Than a Score*; Rick Ayers, *Berkeley High School Slang Dictionary*; Deborah Meier, *The Power of Their Ideas*; and anything by Maxine Greene, starting with *Releasing the Imagination* and *The Dialectic of Freedom*.

Well, damn! I didn't mean to get started, but since I've jumped the fence and gone off road, let me suggest that you read James Baldwin and George Orwell, among the most ambitious ethical writers of the 20th century, and then read a couple more contemporary essayists as well: Edward Said, *Reflections on Exile*; Rebecca Solnit, *Men Explain Things to Me*; Ta-Nehisi Coates, *Between the World and Me*.

For poetry start with Claudia Rankine, *Citizen*; Kevin Coval, *A People's History of Chicago*; and Eve Ewing, *Electric Arches*. And for novels illuminating the lives of young people in and out of school, try Saffire, *Push*; Gish Jen, *Mona in the Promised Land*; Junot Diaz, *The Brief Wondrous Life of Oscar Wao*; Jamaica Kincaid, *Lucy*; Rachel DeWoskin, *Big Girl Small* or *Blind*; Allison Bechdel, *Fun Home*; and Sandra Cisneros, *The House on Mango Street*.

Enough! I'm gasping for air myself!

But you get the idea. Start reading, and keep going.

Not only will you be building a culture of literacy for (and around) yourself, you'll experience (as will your future students) what James Baldwin discovered as a young man: "You think your pain and your heartbreak are unprecedented in the history of the world, but then you read. It was books that taught me that the things that tormented me most were the very things that connected me with all the people who were alive, or who had ever been alive" (goodreads.com/quotes/5853-you-think-your-pain-and-your-heart-break-are-unprecedented-in).

Read! Read! Read!

: : :

Authentic education is always in some ways self-education. Each of us assents to learning certain things; each of us avoids or resists other things. The teacher creates an environment, it's true, offers prompts and prods, challenges and support, stimulation, provocation, and nourishment, but the learner must actively reach out and choose to learn. Watch a toddler learning to walk or talk—it's not the instruction so much as the setting, the support, the encouragement. That kid wants to talk, the motive is intrinsic, and the practice relentless. Our task is critical: assistance and collaboration, spark and affirmation. But the learner's role and action are at the heart of the matter, and her cardinal rule—when she so chooses—is *to reach.*

I mention this here because as you make your twisty way toward teaching, there are countless things that you will learn on your own—seeking out mentors and allies, searching for examples of good teaching, gathering materials/supplies—or you'll have to teach yourself in the absence of formal instruction: self-education. This is in part because so many aspects of teaching are personal and linked to your particular personality and standpoint, and in part because teaching is relational and depends on the character and temperament, position and perspective of everyone gathered together in class. The range of relationships and interactions that unfolds in the classroom is staggering, and staying wide awake to the swirling, tumultuous reality of classroom life as it's being lived is to be in a permanent posture of self-education.

Beyond that there are two competencies that are rarely foregrounded (and sometimes not even mentioned) in teacher education programs that are central to the enterprise and that great teachers attend to and need to master: One is knowing how to create an environment for learning that is deep enough and wide enough to embrace the vast range of actual students (as opposed to some imagined, idealized, and stereotyped "3rd-grader" or "middle schooler") who walk through your door; the other is learning how to observe and record the behaviors, performances, and actions of students as they grow and learn. Each of these skills warrants an entire chapter of its own (below), but I mention them here because there are practical things you can do now, before you enter the classroom, in anticipation of developing these skills as part of your teaching practice going forward.

The environment for learning. Think of the classroom environment as the Third Teacher, right behind a child's parent/caregiver (Teacher 1) and you (Teacher 2). You are the principal creator of the Third Teacher, so you will need to pay close attention to how you intend to build out the physical space, of course, but also how you will establish the tone and the atmosphere that you want in your setting, how you'll fashion an appropriate spirit and aesthetic, and how you plan to shape the psychological feel as well as the logical dimensions of your space.

We'll get into more detail soon, but for now let's make conscious and explicit what you already know intuitively: Every built environment strongly suggests how you're to behave in those spaces. You visit your grandmother and her kitchen itself seems to cry out, "Pull up a chair and start eating!" before she says a word; you enter a friend's apartment and the large couch dominating the front room and facing the TV (which is turned on) and the refrigerator (which is filled with cold beer), and a coffee table with bowls of chips and salsa, tells you most of what you need to know about the main activity expected here; you enter a certain house of worship and the space recommends quiet meditation, while attending a raucous sports event urges you to lose your shit. In a similar way, settings tell you what not to do: Entering a lecture hall, you're not likely to mount the stage, approach the podium, and start talking (even though no one said you couldn't); attending a basketball game, you probably won't take the floor and start doing warm-ups with the Splash Brothers, KD, and Draymond. The environment is a sturdy and persistent instructor.

Starting today, carry a small notebook in your backpack or your vest pocket in order to annotate the environments you come across in your wanderings and your travels. Start with your bedroom or your kitchen, and work out from there. Notice how a nearby park is laid out, what messages it communicates to folks, and see how the airport or the bus or train terminal directs traffic. These places are neither natural nor god-given nor accidental, so imagine who thought it should be just so, and why. Look at a mall or your favorite coffee shop or a shared workspace or a grocery store and, working backwards, reconstruct the thinking and planning that led to this specific result. The point is not that you will necessarily borrow anything from these spaces directly, but rather that you will become more tuned into the fact that every built environment is broadcasting messages, and that each has a tone and an aesthetic, a purpose and a spirit that are the result of human consciousness—for better or for worse.

Observe and record. Seeing your students as whole, three-dimensional human beings, dynamic and in motion, is a challenge you'll face every day as a teacher. Knowing intellectually that they are more than their bodies or their presenting behaviors, knowing that they have hearts and minds, spirits and souls, aspirations and dreams, is not enough. You have to develop the habit of close observation. And then the construction of written accounts of all you see.

A professor walks into the lecture hall. She looks to be well over 60 years old. Her movements are rigid, almost mechanical, and she has a scowl on her face as she walks to the board, takes a piece of chalk from the tray, and writes, "Dr. Lorraine Levinson, Ph.D." You could look more deeply, but why bother? She's so obviously a bitter, burned-out grouch, old-school and deeply conservative. This is likely to be a tiresome class and a complete slog.

But as often happens in everyday life, your hasty conclusion completely outran and obliterated a deeper truth, and your superficial observation was dead wrong. If you'd paid closer attention you might have noticed a back brace beneath her jacket, the top just visible above her collar. You might have seen the walker parked at the entrance to the hall. You might have observed a graduate student arranging the professor's notes and books at the lectern. You will soon discover that your snap judgment was off by about 180 degrees: Professor Levinson ("Please call me Lorraine") is in her 40s and recovering from a difficult back surgery; she's in a lot of pain, but she is, in fact, also remarkably responsive to student concerns, wise and funny and lively, knowledgeable and nurturing. So you were mistaken about her, but no matter—things turned out just fine.

Perhaps. But this casual rush to a simpleminded and erroneous conclusion is typical of each of us in our everyday interactions: Some jerk zooms past you on the highway and rudely cuts in front, so you flip the jerk the bird. You feel entirely self-righteous and justified. But what you didn't know is that the jerk was in a frenzy heading to the ER where her teenage son was just taken following a bike accident.

The point is that we see mostly what's right in front of our faces—how could it be otherwise?—and we often miss the contexts in which particular behaviors or performances are situated. I'm not asking you to catch up with the highway jerk and ask for an explanation, but I will argue that in your classroom and with your students you should develop enough humility that feelings of self-righteousness are resisted or banished, that conclusions are always contingent and tempered with doubt, and that you remind yourself to pause, look more closely, and probe more deeply. This means in part nurturing the disposition of mind and the habit of the heart that allows you to assume your students are doing the best they can given the circumstances of their lives, as well as the curiosity and wonder to rethink, re-examine, re-imagine and rebuild alongside them. It also means developing the skill needed to accurately observe and record human behavior.

> In your classroom and with your students you should develop enough humility that feelings of self-righteousness are resisted or banished, that conclusions are always contingent and tempered with doubt, and that you remind yourself to pause, look more closely, and probe more deeply.

So take that small notebook you're carrying in your backpack or your vest pocket, the one designed to focus your attention on the environments that you encounter, and add another section (or get a second—or is it by now a third?—notebook), this one centered on close observations of people in motion—a waitress at the diner, for example, or a stranger on the train, a cop on his coffee break or a street performer at the shopping center, the manager of a carwash and one of her workers. Fill the notebook up with written sketches and as much thick description as you can muster, and then get another notebook. Keep practicing the fine art of observing and recording.

: : :

Finally, as with most things of importance, look deep within yourself. Access your values and your principles, and get in touch with the intuitions, instincts, and passions that draw you to teach. Spell out your core commitments as a teacher and as a human being, and jot them down so that you have a handy list to consult when the going gets tough. We'll revisit the list—your commitments to your students and yourself—later, but it's not too early to get started on your list right now.

Part of your practice should be regular self-reflection on all kinds of matters of importance: Where do we come from? What are we? Where are we going? What are the circumstances of our lives, and how might they be otherwise? What time do you think it is on the clock of the universe?

What does it mean to love our shared world? What does it mean to be human today? What do you owe to a friend or a neighbor, to a person asking you for spare change outside your favorite coffee shop, or to a proximate stranger? Why? Are you a good person? How do you know you are? How would anyone else know you are? When did you last make a consciously ethical decision? What happened? Given the times we live in, are you an American? What evidence would you produce right now if someone in authority walked in and asked you to prove it? Would you ask that authoritative person for proof of his claim to be an American? Are you free? What's the evidence? How will you live your life right now so as not to make a mockery of your values? How will you know if you're succeeding?

This is more than an empty exercise or an airy gesture. Teachers are the instruments of their own ongoing and evolving practice, and knowing yourself as a complex intellectual and ethical force will illuminate your teaching in spectacular ways. Try it.

CHAPTER : THREE

How Can I Get to
Know My Students?

I'm so glad you asked.

Because this is the first as well as the most formidable and abiding challenge every teacher must face: seeing your students as three-dimensional creatures—much like yourselves—with hearts and minds, spirits and souls, experiences and perspectives, hopes and histories, passions and preferences that must somehow be grasped, appreciated, and taken into account.

New teachers sometimes have difficulty switching the focus to the students and away from themselves—"How am I doing? Did my lesson go well? Do the students like me or think I'm cool?" This line of thinking needs to yield a bit, and move toward a different order of question: How is Britt doing this morning? What does Erin make of this project? Is Jay's energy flagging, and why?

No student should be seen through the frame of a simple one-dimensional label (BD, LD, EMH, GT); every student is more than a brand and more than a score. Each comes to class from a particular family and heritage, a company of ancestors, a specific neighborhood, a community, a culture, a language group, and a network of friends and associates, and that entire ensemble accompanies the student across the threshold into class every day—they're not visible to the naked eye, to be sure, but make no mistake about it, if you pay close enough attention you'll sense now and then that the whole throng is present, crowded together on top of the desk or sharing the chair, hovering in the air above and alongside the student. What fun to realize that your class of 25 or 30 is in fact an audience of thousands!

Teaching is intensely relational work, and you simply cannot build a relationship with someone you don't know, someone who's invisible to you, or someone who is perceived exclusively through the distorted lenses of stereotype and cliché. In order to become the best possible teacher for your students you must investigate and uncover their interests and

Teaching is intensely relational work, and you simply cannot build a relationship with someone you don't know, someone who's invisible to you, or someone who is perceived exclusively through the distorted lenses of stereotype and cliché.

purposes, questions and needs, capabilities and intentions.

Of course our knowledge of any human being is always incomplete, partial, contingent—hell, that's true even when it comes to knowing yourself. There is no knowing for a fact—for teachers, there's only listening, looking, and humility. Each student is her own sovereign state, each an entire universe—vast, expanding, dynamic. If you were to attempt to draw a map of any one of us (again, even yourself) there would necessarily be immense unexplored areas, mysterious magnetic holes, undiscovered continents, evasive mountains concealing hidden lakes and secret passes. We're entirely too big to be mapped, too complex to be captured on anybody's linear statistical printout—or, frankly, on a standardized test. You might conclude, then, that the prospect is fruitless—a fool's errand—and hardly worth your effort. Wrong. The fact that you will never get to the end of it, that you cannot reach bottom, might be a point of misery if your mood is melancholy, but it could, as well, be a cause for infinite delight and even celebration—gathered before you, after all, is humanity itself in all of its wild diversity and magnificent glory, capable of everything and immune to nothing. The fact that you'll never see or understand another human being in full should not divert you from seeing and understanding each student as well as you possibly can, and especially pursuing and apprehending those things that can guide your classroom planning, your teaching strategies, and your daily practice.

Of course it would be unfair in any relationship to relentlessly seek out another's interests and purposes while withholding or masking your own, so be prepared to have your own personal intentions, passions, and preferences accessible and on display as well. Further, be clear in your own heart and mind as well as in your practical approaches that observation in your hands is fully in the service of teaching and learning, and is in no way, shape, or form linked to surveillance—your job description doesn't include spying, inspecting, regulating, or policing. Your aspiration as a teacher is to be a coach and a guide, an instructor and a mentor, a co-learner and a counselor, not an autocratic ruler or an almighty overlord. If you go even a little way down that road it's as if you announced on the first day of class something like this: "Welcome, students! We're going to have a terrific time together this year, a time of growth and learning, exploration and discovery, enjoyment and on most days, hopefully, feelings of deep satisfaction for a job well done . . . But first, let's call the cops."

Don't do that.

Instead, start with an unshakable belief that each student who enters your classroom is a person of incalculable value. Take that belief on faith, meaning that it doesn't have to be proven to you by this or that student, but is based, rather, on the evidence of things not seen. You can hold to that faith in the face of bad behavior, terrible attitude, and in spite of official policy. Your job is not to compute the student's worth—remember: It's incalculable—but to support learning and growth, and to challenge and nurture the inherent desire to keep learning, growing, and moving forward that you believe (on faith!) is alive somewhere inside each one.

You can choose to look at your students through your own curious eyes, your own critical mind, and your own generous heart, despite (or in addition to) the policies and procedures required by your administrators or supervisors. You can resist the alphabet soup of labels that cling to kids like barnacles, sharp and ugly, and resist as well the toxic habit of defining kids by their deficits, even if this is the norm in your school. The school may see Rafe, for example, exclusively as ADD (attention deficit disorder) and that sticky label may put him out of focus in many of his encounters in school, but in your classroom Rafe can also be known to you as PP (phenomenal poet) or HHM (helpful hall monitor). Like everyone else, he's multidimensional, and, yes, he's also a particularly feisty person, but don't allow Rafe (at least in your class) to be trapped in an airless room with no exit. Rafe is complicated, and in transit, the same old Rafe but also a new Rafe in certain ways every day, just like you. You have a mind of your own, so use it—make space for Rafe to be more fully himself; become a student of Rafe's (as well as all of your other students) and learn what you can from him in spite of everything. I think you'll find deep satisfaction as well as endless surprise in this gesture alone.

> You can hold to that faith in the face of bad behavior, terrible attitude, and in spite of official policy. Your job is not to compute the student's worth— remember: It's incalculable.

If your sole teaching strategy is lecturing or writing up and then delivering prefabricated lessons to passive, seemingly obedient students, you're not only denying them the fullest range of intelligences and learning opportunities they might access, you're also, importantly, cutting yourself off from a multitude of occasions when you might see your students as whole, propulsive, high-octane learners. If students are mainly sitting quietly and watching you—the only animated person in sight—you can't learn much about them as learners. We'll return to this later, but for now, note that authentic learning is typically active and energetic—think of your student (or of any learner, really) as an unruly spark of meaning-making energy on a voyage of discovery and surprise.

If you need real-life examples, go to a nearby playground and pick out any child to study—OK, take that 3-year-old over there in the sandbox with a couple of buckets, a cup, and a shovel; she fills one bucket and then the other with sand, walks a few steps away, empties them onto a growing pile, and returns to fill them once more; she notices that two bucketfuls from the little bucket fill the bigger one, and she repeats that experiment several times, practicing until she's confident that she's figured it out; after a while she goes to the fountain and fills her cup with water, which she pours onto the top of the mountain she's just made, tracing the resulting river with her finger; when another toddler comes by, she gives him the cup and they keep working, side by side, chattering away, though not necessarily to one another. This goes on for over half an hour, until her caregiver rounds her up and says it's time to go.

Notice that there is no teacher "teaching" in this scenario, no one wielding an almighty lesson plan, no one lecturing from a podium, and notice, too, that our 3-year-old is not taking notes. She's not (at this point in her life, anyway) anyone's "target of instruction." Nonetheless, she's obviously learning, her motivation coming largely from within herself and prompted by sand and shovel and bucket and water, driving her to make sense and to make meaning, to be busy-busy-busy learning about the going world that she was thrust into a mere 3 years ago, including, for this brief time, learning something about proportion and equivalence, physics and chemistry, language and social interaction, just for starters. Her concentration and enthusiasm are awesome—and no one offered her any shiny reward or chilling punishment to get her up and going.

This is the view with a grain of sand—real learning, happening all around us all the time. We'd surely be clearer and more effective teachers if we paid closer attention to these unruly sparks, noticed how they make sense of the world, and built our own teaching practices within and alongside them.

There will be times when you will need to be front and center in the classroom, but resist the temptation to be there all the time. Make lectures, teacher's talk, and direct instruction short and pointed; make room for collaboration and small-group work, for projects, for partnering up on an assignment, for free-choice time, for performances, and more—all in the interest of promoting self-learning while providing you opportunities to see the children at work and in motion. Early childhood classrooms are typically organized around interest areas: blocks, dress-up or make-believe, math and manipulative materials, book area or library, and art stations including collage and clay and painting. Because kids are choosing and learning actively, teachers have multiple occasions to observe and record the children's strategies, insights, preferences, and know-how. And there's no reason why this way of enhancing the visibility of learners learning has to disappear after the 3rd grade.

A 5th-grade teacher I know has interest areas like a kindergarten, but modified for 10-year-olds—reference books in one corner, art materials in a designated cabinet, map-making area, weaving and sewing stations, math materials including Cuisenaire rods and geo-boards, chess and checkers center, and more—and lots of time for students to work independently. Our son Malik teaches middle school math, and while he offers direct instruction—what he calls "mini-lectures"—when needed, he immediately sets students to work on sets of problems (often using counting boards, buttons, marbles, abacuses) in groups of six, with this caveat: "Work together and help one another understand the concept, and only come to me if all six of you have the same question." In other words, he's asking them to cooperate, collaborate, and teach one another, while he moves from group to group observing and noticing. (A cynic might say he's incentivizing cheating! Nonsense.) When a group finishes the problem set, they can work independently or in small groups on art projects or with board games (his collection is vast, assembled over years of teaching).

But keep reminding yourself that each of your students is a three-dimensional creature, a singular character who will walk the earth but once, forging a twisty, one-of-a-kind track across the landscape. Each learns idiosyncratically, that is, in a style, pace, and sequence all their own. Your work is to discover that style, that pace. Each is the one-of-one—entirely unique and uniquely capable. Get in touch with that reality and resist anything that sees children only in the aggregate while obliterating the individual learner. To treat anyone like a thing, to attempt to own or exploit or oppress another, is, of course, a first-order moral mistake; so is objectifying or attaching a label to a student. I reject the idea that students can be known by either their worst behavior or their statistical profiles—age, gender, race, ethnicity, zip code—and I support the refusal of young people to submit to that kind of regimen in school.

To treat anyone like a thing, to attempt to own or exploit or oppress another, is, of course, a first-order moral mistake; so is objectifying or attaching a label to a student. I reject the idea that students can be known by either their worst behavior or their statistical profiles—age, gender, race, ethnicity, zip code—and I support the refusal of young people to submit to that kind of regimen in school.

You might begin each year with a one-on-one interview with each child during free or activity time. A 2nd-grade teacher I know does this during the daily 30-minute silent reading time, and learns a lot that will help her as the class proceeds. She has a schedule of questions like these: "What was the best thing about kindergarten, and about first grade? What do you hope second grade will be like? Are there any special projects you'd like to work on this year? Who do you know who's a great reader, and what do they like to read?"

She begins class with a name song ("The Name Game," "Who Stole the Cookie from the Cookie Jar?") and every name is mentioned to start each day. Every week she has a designated corner of the room for the "Student of the Week," where a different child is featured each Monday with photos, toys or games or artifacts from home, and another, longer interview: favorite foods, best-loved books, sports, things that make you happy, how you got your first name, and more. The Student of the Week offers an "I-search" display, something about that the student researched, like the story of their grandparents' early life in another country or in another part of the United States. On Friday the Student of the Week sits by the display and takes questions from the other students.

Students can learn in your class how to grapple—both now and in the future—with a question central to the spirit and heart of democracy, a question both simple and profound, straightforward and twisty: What's your story? How will you find a voice in which to tell it fully and fairly?

All human life, of course, is in part a story of suffering, loss, and pain. When that pain is preventable, the suffering undeserved, we object, and in our opposition is another commonplace in our human story. Sometimes students' stories are ignored or diminished by others, sometimes they're seen exclusively through the distorting frame of stereotypes and labels, their undeniable and indispensable three-dimensionality suffocated and diminished, their hopes handcuffed and their possibilities policed. The development of a more powerful and compelling voice becomes even more essential.

Who are you in the world? What in the world are your chances and your choices? How is your story like or unlike other stories? What's next? What is it you plan to do, as the poet Mary Oliver urges, with your one wild and precious life? What are the next chapters going to be, and the chapters after that, and after that? No one knows for sure, for each person must write those next chapters—and even so, only partially, for every life is also a dance of the dialectic, a sometimes difficult negotiation between chance and choice.

In finding their voices and telling their stories, students can rely on you—their smart and sensitive teacher—to acknowledge and appreciate their minds and their spirits, their perspectives and their lived experiences. You can help lift them up and beyond the negative and the controlling.

Malik taught English as a Second Language (ESL) for a few years, and he began each class session with a 5-minute free write based on a provocation that emerged from some discussion in class or from his large (and growing) folder of prompts. These include: (1) Everybody always asks me . . . ; (2) What's your mother's name and where is she from? What's your mother's mother's name, and where is she from? What's your name, and how did you get here?; (3) What were the circumstances of your birth?; (4) Have you ever been wrongly accused?; (5) Write a 6-word memoir; and 6) Tell your life story in 60 seconds. No one is required to share aloud, but in just a few minutes a few folks are typically willing to read their pieces—"no editing; no apologies and no backsies"— and the results are variously hilarious, poignant, illuminating, and wise. As the class took up the day's reading, Malik moved around the room working on grammar, spelling, usage, and vocabulary with each student based on her own free write.

Hopes and dreams and most fears are childish, as is all art and storytelling. Still, it's what we have at hand: The world is made up of stories. Nothing more—just stories and stories about stories. Telling their stories, trusting their stories, listening actively and empathetically to the stories of others—this is all part of the work of democracy. Everyone counts, and nobody counts more than any one else. True in the larger world, and a central truth in your classroom practice.

CHAPTER : FOUR

How Do I Create an
Outstanding Learning Environment?

Field trip!

I was a new teacher, and so I didn't give it a minute's consideration: Someone suggested a class trip to the city airport, and my instant response was: Yes!! So a week later—without any thought and with absolutely no planning—I found myself at the mouth of Concourse A with a large and lovely group of 5-year-olds in tow. What happened next was a shock and a surprise to me: The children took off racing down the concourse at full speed as if a starting bell (that I alone failed to hear) had sounded and the racers knew exactly what to do. Pandemonium! Kids running fast and faster, their inexperienced and hapless teacher (me) trying to round them up and pull the group back together.

Back at school I explained—calmly and reasonably, I hoped—that they could not run around and away from me on a field trip. To be safe and productive, and to be welcomed into a public space, we had to stay together, hold hands, behave well, and watch out for one another. They nodded in unison and seemed to understand.

Next time we ventured to the airport I was confident that we were all well prepared. The children knew the rules, each one was paired with a partner, and each was outfitted with a small notebook and colored pencils to record memorable moments on the trip. As we approached Concourse A, all instruction and rational thought flew out the window, and they took off speeding down the straightaway with me, once again, in pursuit. My assessment of our readiness was all wrong.

Or was it? Something else was going on, and although it took me several experiences (and accompanying miscalculations) to get it, I slowly realized that the problem was not in our preparations, but rather in my failure to see what was right in front of me: The environment itself was acting as a

powerful instructor, and it was contradicting my message (Stick together . . .
Don't run . . .) with a more compelling message of its own: Run!!!

The third teacher asserted itself.

This happened long ago, and yet I revisit the experience whenever I
think of the importance of creating an environment for learning. I was
only 20 years old, and I'd just grasped a principal lesson about teaching
that would guide me for a lifetime: The third teacher is fundamental—in
some instances almighty—and you ignore it at your peril. I elaborated on
and deepened that lesson over time, and I've never since looked casually at
a human-made environment—I probe each of them for their intended and
unintended meanings, their explicit and implicit instructions, their plans
and aspirations, tone and feel. The third teacher can be your best friend and
trusted ally, or your adversary and opponent. It's really up to you.

Years later I spent many months in the school at the juvenile jail in
Chicago, where I worked with several committed and inspiring teachers.
Mr. B was one of the best, and he was especially attuned to creating an environment that would do some of the heavy lifting in terms of his teaching
goals for these youth. His students were all young men, 15 and 16 years old,
charged with serious crimes, and awaiting trials in adult criminal court.
There would be no opportunities for field trips for this teacher.

One might have expected a military-style classroom—no-nonsense,
hierarchical and autocratic, strict discipline on full display. Mr. B had the
opposite approach: The front door was adorned with a big WELCOME sign,
along with pictures of each student accompanied by a few autobiographical
comments: "Marcus: I'm fifteen, and I love the Bulls."

The classroom had brightly colored prints of famous paintings on every wall—Picasso's "Guernica" and "Les Demoiselles d'Avignon," Klimt's
"The Kiss," Van Gogh's "The Starry Night," Munch's "The Scream"—with
an entire designated space for several reproductions from Mr. B's favorite
painter, Jacob Lawrence, which included select pieces from the Migration,
Harriet Tubman, Frederick Douglass, and John Brown series. The room was
bright and beautiful, a distinct line being drawn by Mr. B between *here*, our
vital shared classroom space, and *there*, whatever difficult realities might lie
right outside of here. Mr. B had classical music playing softly on his boom
box much of the day, and always as the students arrived each morning; he
insisted that "high culture" belonged to everyone, and that "the only thing
standing between Bach and my boys is opportunity." It surprised me one
day—though it shouldn't have—when a student asked Mr. B to put on the
Goldberg Variations.

There were four easels with paint trays along one wall; a workbench, basic tools, and a bin of wood in one corner; and the classroom library overflowing with books and magazines and newspapers in another. During free time students could choose to work in one of these areas, or play games or work away at ongoing bookmaking projects at the long table in the back of the class. The desks were set up in pairs so that each student had a partner during "instruction time," when Mr. B would lead a discussion or present a lesson—this was a self-contained classroom, so he taught everything from math and science to English and history with a group that had wildly different levels of skill and achievement. He proceeded with the given curriculum, modifying it where he saw that it was needed, but his heart was in free time, where he could encourage imagination and creativity as he monitored the needs and progress of his students.

Mr. B wanted his young men to learn to work together, to cooperate, to make choices, and he wanted each of them to have the experience of creating something original at the easels or the workbench or the writing table. He wanted them to feel respected and treated with calm kindness for no other reason than that they're human beings, part of the human family and worthy, therefore, of a certain human reverence. He hoped his class would help them to be more fully in touch with their humanness. Every Friday Mr. B broke an institution-wide rule by bringing doughnuts from Dunkin' Donuts for midmorning snack, not as a reward, but as a gesture of caring. "These are teenage boys," he would say with a laugh. "Hungry all the time, and in these circumstances, eating institutional food and feeling especially deprived on every level, hunger is a massive metaphor. It's so easy for me to pick up doughnuts, and it means so much to them—their outsized gratitude is both flattering and embarrassing. Why wouldn't I do it?"

⋮　⋮　⋮

Think for a moment about classrooms you experienced as a kid. What do you remember about how the classroom looked, the tone and the feel, the sense of comfort or discomfort? Did any of your classrooms boom out the message "READ!"? Did any say, "Make Yourself at Home" or "Create" or "Be Curious"? How did they do that? And think about classrooms you've looked at more recently. What messages were embedded in those spaces? How did the teachers accomplish that work? Finally, look at your college classrooms, and ask the same questions. Are those spaces intentionally working as third teachers? How and why, or why not? With a couple of notable exceptions—Bank Street College, the Workshop Center at the City College of New York— in my experience college classrooms have been typically bare rectangles with fluorescent lighting, nondescript institutional paint jobs, and bad air, but perhaps your experience is different. If so, how?

One year, teaching a course called "Improving Learning Environments" at the University of Illinois at Chicago, I felt an intense contradiction between the content of our curriculum and classroom conversation, and the reality of our meeting place. The classroom was built theater-style, with unmovable banks of chairs and foldout tabletops on escalating risers, a podium on a small stage, and no windows. The venue itself sent all the wrong messages from my perspective, and I despised it, so I plotted to disrupt and *improve* it—we would not simply speak abstractly about improving learning environments, we would take this dreadful space as a challenge, and make it at least a little better.

The first night, after complaining about the horrible lighting, I asked each student to bring an alternative source of illumination to our second class meeting the following week. The result was marvelous: candles in a vast range of sizes and shapes, a variety of flashlights, a few LED headlamps, an Aladdin lamp, lava lamp, Coleman camping lantern, glow sticks, snap lights, a wooden sconce that held a large candle surrounded by mirrors on three sides, and a homemade oil lamp made from a Mason jar, household twine, and canola oil. We turned off the fluorescent overheads, fired up the alternatives, and the symphony of light was dazzling, warm, and comforting. We left whatever objects students could live without in the room after class.

It was so successful that I asked folks to bring a living thing to our next class meeting, and students came with offerings of plants and trees, an herb garden, an ant farm and a worm pile, a bowl of fish, a ferret and a hamster, and two kittens. WOW!! This icky classroom was getting better and better. Again, we left behind whatever students could comfortably donate (not the cats, ferret, or hamster), our little improvements in place for other students in other classes to enjoy.

And so it went, week after week. Let's create a class library in this area— BOOM! Books and graphics and magazines filled the room. Let's make this place reflective of who we are: Autobiographical sketches were hung from the walls along with photo collages and "cultural artifacts" brought from home. Our improvements and designs sprouted everywhere, spilling out into the hallway and colonizing all available space.

We were so energized and so excited by disrupting and changing this space that we thoughtlessly lost sight of our impact on others (including the custodial staff) until a dear friend and colleague whose class met in the same room on a different night jokingly sent a message through our shared students: "Tell Professor Ayers to get that shit out of my classroom." Oops! We reluctantly disassembled our good work, impressed nonetheless with what a few simple gestures could do to transform a seemingly intractable room into something bristling with life and learning. That was a lesson worth remembering.

: : :

The starting point for creating your own specific classroom environment is to focus on how children learn—which is light-years away from the pervasive and dominant "banking model," in which teachers make deposits of knowledge and information into open slots in the heads of inanimate students who are about as lively as ceramic piggy banks. This model belies everything we know about how human beings actually learn. Learning is active, not passive; social and interactive, not individual; natural, not exceptional. The deep motivation to learn is instinctive, innate, inborn.

Watch any toddler for 10 minutes: All five senses are fully engaged as he careens through the playground or preschool or living room, observing, listening, touching, smelling, tasting. You might want to create a space, even for much older kids, that triggers all five senses. Little kids—all youth, really—are in motion and in action; they're not sitting still and being quiet, the misguided but typical prerequisite to "learning" in school. They are profoundly social and naturally interactive, chattering away with other toddlers, friends and classmates, family members, and all manner of adults. Look more closely: They're building, creating, performing, imagining, as well as pursuing projects where they can hypothesize, experiment, test out, question, express themselves—all in the interest of constructing knowledge and making meaning, that is, they're *learning*. And parenthetically, if you're ever having an existential crisis, wondering about the meaning of life, go observe toddlers for a day and you'll find the answer—the meaning of life is to live!

Children are also constantly interacting with the environment itself, something Loris Malaguzzi, a psychologist working with families in Reggio Emilia, Italy, after World War II, designated the "third teacher." If we think of the environment that way—as the third teacher—it's super-exciting news: We now have a classroom assistant who's always been there, but is too often ignored or taken for granted. We should all be smarter and more fully conscious in the ways that we now construct and deploy that assistant teacher—you can wake up and get busy building a more vital and spirited relationship with your new friend, that third teacher.

> Whatever and whomever you teach, and whatever else you do, make sure your environment adheres to the well-known and often-cited physicians' oath: First, do no harm.

Whatever and whomever you teach, and whatever else you do, make sure your environment adheres to the well-known and often-cited physicians' oath: First, do no harm. I also like the related advice of Joe Maddon, the manager of the Chicago Cubs: Try not to suck. Your space should be safe, respectful, and enjoyable. And it should also allow students to move and make real choices, to interact with one another, to build, create, perform, invent, imagine, wonder, daydream, fidget, hypothesize, experiment, test out, question, and express themselves in a variety of ways. Don't spend your time vainly trying to coerce students to be silent and immobile—it's unnatural, and, more to the point, it's simply not how humans learn most of the time.

Most of the time people learn best through their own experiences and when they have some control over the direction of their learning. They need to be allowed to explore, with numerous ways to express themselves. Even the youngest children are bearers of knowledge based on their lived lives, and they need to have multiple opportunities to share and refine their thoughts and ideas about everything they encounter and experience during the day. They should be thought of as active apprentices rather than as targets of instruction.

The environment for learning is, of course, more than the physical space; it's also the cultural, social, psychological, emotional space, and these dimensions are also in your hands in a zillion ways you'll have to discover and deploy. As a teacher from preschool through graduate school, I've always begun class by singing a song or reading a poem. With young kids the songs are name songs to begin, branching into folk music and group rounds or sing-alongs. With older students we simply reflect quietly for a moment in response to a poem read aloud, and then typically do a free write. With all ages the opening ritual always involves a short meeting where we look backward and forward in anticipation of today's goals and routines.

You might decide to make the classroom itself—your learning environment—an object of study with your students, something akin to what I did with my college students in that one class. Look around: Is this the classroom we want? How could it better reflect our backgrounds and our particular cultures and subcultures? How could it indicate more strongly our preferences, our goals, our priorities? Is it agile and flexible enough to reflect our changing needs and desires as the year proceeds?

One of my former students led his 5th-graders on an inquiry that ballooned into a yearlong investigation into the condition of their urban public school, and how it compared to nearby private, parochial, and other public schools. Along the way they interviewed teachers, students, neighbors, parents, and public officials, studied environmental impact, and learned about both green and universal design. They spent time with the custodians and designed a coordinated plan in which students could strategically and collectively work to clean up after themselves in certain spaces, freeing the custodial staff for deeper and more long-lasting work to keep the school safe and healthy.

What are 100 ways you could make your space more literate? Word walls, composition corner, author of the week, clippings from newspapers, word-of-the-day? One 3rd-grade teacher I know made a ginormous bookworm, starting with a smiling green worm's head drawn on construction paper taped to the wall. Each time a student read a book, he or she cut a large circle from colored construction paper, wrote the title and author and a one-sentence review, signed it, and taped the segment to the ever-growing worm. When the worm circled the room twice, it headed out the door and down the hall toward the principal's office.

Or maybe you want to get into maps, become map-literate, and find creative ways to understand and represent space visually, first by mapping your own school or neighborhood, your trip to the museum, your bedrooms or kitchens, and then the city playgrounds, parks, and recreation areas. You might collect bus and subway maps of the public transit system, consumer maps made by big retailers, power-use maps created by the gas and electric services, world maps from different historical periods and different perspectives (the Mercator projection next to the Peters Projection Map—same world, wildly different representations), national and state and city maps. Here's one place (among gazillions) where you stand at the intersection of art and science, imagination and fact.

One high school teacher friend in Chicago uses maps and mapping as a primary teaching device, and all kinds of student-made maps are put on display every year. I was particularly taken with an ongoing project that begins with a blank outline of Chicago that students use to map their lives, often multiple times. Some of the maps are crowded and frenzied, some

One map had three entries ("Places I've lived—Mt. Greenwood, Rogers Park, Little Italy"); another had a single dot ("74th and ML King, where the cops pulled me over threw all my stuff in the gutter, ripped out my back seat, and drove off").

descriptive, some more evocative. One map had three entries ("Places I've lived—Mt. Greenwood, Rogers Park, Little Italy"); another had a single dot ("74th and ML King, where the cops pulled me over threw all my stuff in the gutter, ripped out my back seat, and drove off"); one was impressionistic with brown, black, yellow and white filling the entire space and called "Segregated City"; another with areas labeled "Places Not to Go." One kid made a map of the best places to dumpster-dive, another of every train yard he'd ever invaded and tagged. Our friend Aaron Hughes, an antiwar veteran and visual artist, made a map with seven squares representing the homes of leading antiwar vets and a caption reading, "Dear FBI: to save you the hard work of finding where Iraq Veterans Against the War members live, I've made you this map. Stop us now before we end the war."

Make your classroom a museum of culture filled with evocative objects brought from each student's home. Or build an artist's studio or a performance space. You may want to display student work to the public. You'll likely want to have designated spaces that students can decorate or design—cubbies or lockers, a work folder for each—to hold their belongings. You might want to grow your own avocados or mint or basil or catnip or potatoes—if not a full vegetable garden—at the side of the school building.

Think of a classroom that mirrors a home: soft spaces or nests to sit or curl up in, cupboards for snacks, maybe a space for "cool cooking." One classroom I know has a small section of rug at the entrance, and students are asked to take off their shoes and put on their slippers upon entering.

On and on. Honor children, honor their ways of being, their approaches to learning. Start making lists so that a year from now, if your favorite teacher or school supervisor walks into your room, they will know instantly what you value, how you understand children and learning, and what is expected of your students and yourself in this classroom. What would I know about you as a teacher a year or two from now if I—a perfect stranger—came for a visit? What would the third teacher tell me about you and this class? Whatever it is, the kids will see it, feel it, and take it in the moment they walk through your door. Be conscious and deliberate.

CHAPTER : FIVE

What Is My Role
in Curriculum-Making?

Here are a few simple sentences using the familiar word "curriculum":

> Please get together with the other 3rd-grade teachers and design a more up-to-date language arts *curriculum*.

> Your assignment is to create a *curriculum* for high school students about a contemporary social problem.

> Should we develop a *curriculum* about the Civil Rights Movement?

> Here is the advanced middle school math *curriculum* that the central office ordered for next year.

In each instance *curriculum* points toward subject matter, a course of study, perhaps, or a specified plan of instruction. The curriculum in these examples is something concrete and material; it implies an object with linear dimensions and more or less straight lines, everything pretty much settled and static. None of that is surprising: Whenever our conversations turn toward curriculum, most people assume we're discussing this kind of thing, that is, the *intended or stated curriculum*, the disciplines and the subjects, the classes and the readings, all the proposed content to be conveyed from a teacher—with more or less creativity, more or less strict adherence to the mandates—to a group of students.

But there are a few serious problems here: If teachers focus solely on the intended curriculum, the classroom becomes anemic, teacher agency and creativity are reduced to nothing more than an added book or two, a clever project or some decoration within the given frame, and everyone's vision is precipitously narrowed to one aspect of school life at the expense of many others. True, this intended curriculum is the obvious stuff of mission

> If teachers focus solely on the intended curriculum, the classroom becomes anemic, teacher agency and creativity are reduced to nothing more than an added book or two, a clever project or some decoration within the given frame, and everyone's vision is precipitously narrowed

statements and policy directives, but it barely scratches the surface when it comes to the everyday questions and challenges teachers face—and the interventions we can wisely make—when we consider *curriculum* in sturdier frames and larger contexts.

My friend and colleague Bill Schubert has thought as deeply and thoroughly about curriculum as anyone I've ever known or read, and he argues that considerations of curriculum ought to begin with what he calls the fundamental curriculum question: What knowledge and experiences are of most value? A thousand adjunct questions follow: How can students gain access to that valuable knowledge and those worthwhile experiences? If a student accomplishes a learning goal, doesn't a new learning goal—a new most valuable bit of knowledge or experience—heave into view? How can one teacher respond to the dynamic of learning agendas constantly growing and changing, or of wildly divergent priorities and preferences and expressions between students of what's taken to be valuable? In other words, isn't it likely that the learning agenda and valuable knowledge for one student is not identical to the valuable knowledge for 30 other students? And if each has a slightly different learning agenda, isn't bedlam looming up ahead?

The fundamental curriculum question reveals something of the real complexity of classroom life, and illuminates part of the deep intellectual challenge every teacher faces. But there's more. Some educators find it helpful in practical terms to consider the curriculum as a dynamic interaction of four "commonplaces"—teachers, learners, subject matter, and milieu—the curriculum consisting of the impact of each on the others. So mathematics does not float abstractly in the air without regard to teachers, learners, and milieu; and the teacher is not a rote performer without regard to subject matter, milieu, and the students themselves; and so on. Teachers needs to be wide awake as they attempt to take a four-eyed approach, attending to each and all in active and vigorous relationship to each and all of the others.

Other educators visualize the curriculum as a matrix, a three-dimensional interaction with 25 variables in three categories: purpose (intellectual, emotional, physical, social, cultural, and more), substance (math, science, history, literature, and so on) and practice (circumstances—who, when, how, what—governance, cost, and so on). Whew! Complicated and mind-boggling, no?

Furthermore, the "intended curriculum" is linked to the ever-present "tested curriculum" but might be dramatically different from the "taught curriculum," which can vary from the stated curriculum in large or small ways depending on things like the personality, choices, and emphasis of the teacher. The "taught curriculum" is different from the "experienced curriculum," which points to how students' prior experiences and knowledge meet the curriculum as stated and presented, and create, then, various (and likely different) experiences for each student. As you try to get your arms around this vast panorama, you might also consider the "embodied curriculum," those things that stay with learners long after school is over; the "out-of-school curriculum," or the impact of things like media, city, neighborhood, family, social relationships, music, hobbies, jobs; the "null or excluded curriculum," things that are not taught, like the arts, for example, in many schools; and the nearly invisible (to adults) "clandestine curriculum," the insider slang and language, culture and shared meanings that students participate in enthusiastically with one another.

Every classroom has as well a huge, often unacknowledged "hidden curriculum," the teaching and learning of assumptions, values, and beliefs not always openly intended or explicitly stated, and rarely considered curriculum at all, but centrally important to the lives of students in school and beyond. The "hidden curriculum" includes things like politeness and respect, or cut-throat competition, obedience, and conformity—I'm reluctant to call these side effects because they're super-strong and often have lasting impacts. All those unstated norms, beliefs, and values undergird the culture and the structure of every school, and work their own mighty will. Because the hidden curriculum is opaque and unavailable for comment or critique, it's often an even more powerful teacher than the official and planned curriculum.

In some places (but I hope not in your class) the essential lessons from the hidden curriculum include passivity in the face of teacher authority, a focus on right answers rather than critical thought, the acceptance of uncritical rote learning and recall as major intellectual achievements, the practice of pretending subject matters are discreet and

In some places (but I hope not in your class) the essential lessons from the hidden curriculum include passivity in the face of teacher authority, a focus on right answers rather than critical thought, the acceptance of uncritical rote learning and recall as major intellectual achievements . . .

separate and that major subjects (math and history) count more than minor subjects (art), the rejection of personal feelings or independent judgment during class time, and the gathering of sometimes random and unrelated facts as the goal of education.

The hidden curriculum may teach about hierarchy and your place in it, indifference, emotional and intellectual dependency, provisional self-esteem, and the requirement that each of us submit to certified authorities. The hidden curriculum may further teach that bells rule supreme, that bodily functions like going to the toilet are enacted on a schedule, that ridicule and shaming are legitimate forms of social interaction. The hidden curriculum might also tell kids that nothing of real importance is ever undertaken, nothing is ever connected to anything else, nothing is ever pursued to its deepest limits, nothing is ever finished, and nothing is ever done with investment and courage.

Or the hidden curriculum might communicate to students that official learning is boring, and that school itself is boring, too. No one really believes anymore that all kids will learn the same things in the same ways at the same time, nor that discrete bits of information poured into the heads of inert youngsters will add up to an education, but the boring system grinds on and on, hour after hour, day after boring day, week after week, for months—the big wheel keeps on turning while the life is sucked out of students and teachers alike.

Everyone knows that a lot about school is boring. I know it, you know it. Because you're reading this page, you likely succeeded in school—and in order to have done so you submitted to a lot of boring stuff. I know I did. The work was stupid or irrelevant, repetitive or disconnected—it was boring. And yet you or your family or your community, or all that and more, convinced you that if you ate all the crap on the plate there would be a payoff someday, and look, here you are. You submitted, you were bored, you ingested the curriculum including the hidden curriculum, and it's part of you (and me).

The hidden curriculum is riddled with all manner of problems, but here's one that really jumped out at me: The vice chancellor for communications at Louisiana State University, an educated man from a respected institution of higher learning, said, "I have an advanced degree in communications, but that doesn't qualify me to comment on the New York Philharmonic." No? Why not? In his categorical scheme of things we must wait passively for some authority, someone with an advanced degree in . . . what?—Appreciation? Composition? Performance?—to tell us what we think of the New York Philharmonic. Everything chopped to bits, the cult of the certified expert triumphant.

Education is bold, adventurous, creative, vivid, and illuminating. In other words, education is for explorers, thinkers, and citizens. Clearly, too many schools have little to do with education. Training is for slaves, for loyal subjects, for tractable employees, and for "good soldiers." Education tears down walls; training is all barbed wire.

> Education is bold, adventurous, creative, vivid, and illuminating. In other words, education is for explorers, thinkers, and citizens. Clearly, too many schools have little to do with education.

Clearly the intended curriculum is not the only thing for you to attend to or to focus on as a teacher. Your role in curriculum-making is to understand that curriculum is an embodiment, not merely a unit of study, and to become as aware as possible of every aspect of classroom life, and every dimension and expression of this riotous and unruly curriculum cacophony. You should work to create the "hidden curriculum" deliberately; account for the "out-of-school curriculum" consciously; think about ways to overcome and compensate for the "null curriculum"; and so on. It's not neat and orderly and it's not entirely manageable, but if you pay attention you'll become better and better at riding the curriculum wave that's washing over every classroom and every school all the time.

And, as noted earlier, if you begin with an intentional and abiding faith in your students, if you believe in their innate capacity to learn, to create things, to grow, and to make meaning, if you believe each is capable of both individual and social transformation, curriculum becomes a form of reinventing, re-creating, and re-inscribing—of finding

> Curriculum, then, is a dialogical process in which everyone participates actively as equals—a turbulent, raucous, unpredictable, noisy, and participatory affair, expression and knowledge emerging from the continual interaction of reflection and activity.

voice—a task that can be accomplished only by free subjects, never by inert objects. Curriculum, then, is a dialogical process in which everyone participates actively as equals—a turbulent, raucous, unpredictable, noisy, and participatory affair, expression and knowledge emerging from the continual interaction of reflection and activity.

: : :

Schools built for the early industrial age too often look and function like little factories, and the metaphor of production dominates the discourse—assembly lines, management and supervision, quality control, productivity, and outputs. Students are the raw materials moving dumbly down the assembly line, and curriculum is the bits of value added to the kids by the workers/teachers. A pretty barren and unhappy landscape, underpinned by a near-universal assumption that schools are in the business of sorting and labeling—winners and losers, smart and stupid, good and bad. The good and the smart will walk the runway to the winner's circle, the bad and the stupid will be cast down and out—losers forever. This is a foundational lesson that many schools teach to every/body every day: There is simply no room to recognize the unique qualities of each child nor to support the growth, development, and progress of each; there is little or no attention to curriculum as anything more than what is mandated and then tested.

School learning becomes a commodity, something to be traded in the marketplace like boots and hammers. Unlike boots and hammers, whose value is inherently satisfying and grasped directly and intuitively, the value and use of school learning are elusive and indirect—hence, students are asked to accept its unspecified value on faith and to be motivated and rewarded externally. The value of the curriculum, we're assured, has been calculated precisely by wise and accomplished people, and the masters know better than you (or anyone else) what's best for you. The payoff is way down the line, but it's surely there, somewhere, over the rainbow. "Take this medicine," students are told over and over again, day after tedious day, "it's good for you." Refuse the bitter pill, and go stand in the corner—where all the other losers are assembled. Of course, if you were to point out that lots of dropouts did OK for themselves—Abraham Lincoln and Benjamin Franklin and Frederick Douglass for starters, Herman Melville, Mark Twain, Joseph Conrad, and Lana and Lilly Wachowski as well, and John D. Rockefeller and Andrew Carnegie for good measure—you'd be called an impudent troublemaker, and put in the corner for sure.

There are zillions of curriculum ideas and plans that you can take off the shelf and put to immediate use. Some are worth studying to give you ideas to grow your own. For example, I learned a lot recently from an encounter with a course of study developed by a group affiliated with Black Lives Matter called *Operation Ghetto Storm: 2012 Annual Report on the Extrajudicial Killings of Black People*. The curriculum guide was called "We Charge Genocide Again" and it began by noting that in 2012 police killed

malleable v. *static*

more than 313 Black people nationally—one every 28 hours—and that the use of deadly force against Black people was standard practice, woven into the fabric of society. The group's objective was to have teacher-students and student-teachers engage the realities of extrajudicial killing of Black people with critical thinking and analysis. They encouraged folks to use the curriculum as a malleable menu, not a definitive or static statement.

The best ongoing source I know for curriculum ideas is the teachers' journal from Milwaukee, *Rethinking Schools.* They have thoughtful and useful curriculum guides available for *Rethinking Columbus, Rethinking Bilingual Education, A People's Curriculum for the Earth, Teaching for Black Lives, Rethinking Mathematics, Rethinking Popular Culture and Media, Unlearning "Indian" Stereotypes, Rethinking Sexism, Gender, and Sexuality,* and a lot more. Check them out, and feed your teaching brain.

I'd be remiss if I failed to mention Rick Ayers' *A Teacher's Guide to Studs Terkel's* Working—a really thoughtful and thorough piece by my brilliant younger brother.

: : :

In many ways Martin Luther King, Jr. was the emblematic practitioner of curriculum as public space. He enacted and embodied a curriculum of justice, and he performed on a vast stage—indeed, his classroom was all of society. He asked in a thousand ways what was of most value, what was fair and just; he urged voyages and transformations for himself and for participants in the Movement and for all within the sound of his voice or the sight of his activities; he grew and changed as conditions evolved and developed.

Curriculum is, of course, never neutral—it always has a value, a position, and a politics. For humanists, the value of education and curriculum is its identity with the general quest for human enlightenment and human liberation. Its driving principle is the unity of all humanity, the conviction that every human being is of incalculable value, entitled to decent and universal standards concerning freedom and justice and education, and that any violations, deliberate or inadvertent, must be resisted.

The relationship among education, curriculum, and freedom is deep, intrinsic, and profound—they are in many ways the same thing, as each concerns itself with the fullest expression of human development. To the extent that people reflect upon their lives and become more conscious of themselves as actors in the world, when they ask themselves what knowledge and experience are of most value, they insert themselves as subjects in history, constructors of the human world, and they enact and express themselves, then, as free human beings.

Curriculum as public space can be thought of as an attempt to broaden the sense of education in such a way that every member of society can develop and use all of his or her capacities and powers without infringing upon the basic conditions or rights of others. The classroom—society itself—becomes an association in which the free development of each is the condition for the free development of all.

> Curriculum and education are arenas of struggle as well as hope—struggle because they stir in us the need to look at the world anew . . . and hope because they gesture toward the future, toward the impending, toward the coming of the new.

Curriculum and education are arenas of struggle as well as hope—struggle because they stir in us the need to look at the world anew, to question what we have created, to wonder what is worthwhile for human beings to know and experience—and hope because they gesture toward the future, toward the impending, toward the coming of the new. This is where we ask how we might engage, enlarge, and change our lives, and it is, then, where we confront our dreams and struggle over notions of the good life, where we try to comprehend, apprehend, or possibly even change the world. Curriculum as public space is a natural site of contestation—sometimes restrained, other times in full eruption—over questions of justice.

I return again and again to a model curriculum that has inspired and instructed me for ages—the *1964 Mississippi Freedom School Curriculum*, based in the historic Civil Rights Movement. It's unlike any curriculum you've ever seen, but it is a published curriculum that you can access and study for ideas about curriculum-making in your own context.

In 1963 a young civil rights worker proposed to create a network of Freedom Schools across the South as a way to re-energize and re-focus the Civil Rights Movement. He noted that while Black people had been denied many things—decent facilities, fully trained teachers, forward-looking curriculum—the fundamental injury was a denial of the right to "think for themselves" about the conditions of their lives, how they came to be the way they were, and how they might be changed. This initiated a public curriculum of questions: Why are we in the Freedom Movement? What do we want that we don't have? What do we have that we want to keep? Pursuing these questions, teachers taught the 3Rs and so much more: how to take oneself seriously as a thinking person; how to locate one's life in the contexts of culture and history, political power and economic condition; how to imagine and then actively work toward a new and improved society.

Over the next several years Freedom Schools were launched all over the country, and not just in schools, but in community centers as well, in churches, parks, coffee shops—in fact, in any space where people gathered together to face one another in dialogue. It was sometimes wild and unruly, always noisy and diverse, and yet it had several common edges: Teachers and leaders became students of their students, the extraordinary ordinary people; students were active participants in their own learning rather than the inert and passive receptacles of someone else's ideas; consumers became citizens and objectified people transformed themselves into subjects and history-makers; teaching and learning were recast as having a larger purpose than occupational training—the fullest participation possible in the world we share, including the development of capacities to change ourselves and to change that world. People got a taste then of curriculum as public space, curriculum characterized by its open access and its propulsive midwifery properties.

With all this in mind, my inspiring teacher/brother Rick Ayers has what he calls "a simple formula"—simple to say while excruciatingly difficult to enact: (1) a community that's engaged, and (2) a curriculum that's engaging.

CHAPTER : SIX

What Is My Part in
Student Assessment in an Era
of High-Stakes Standardized Testing?

Whether you like it or not, you'll likely be required to administer high-stakes standardized tests at some point in the year. Perhaps often. It's not particularly useful to you as a teacher, it's not authentic assessment, and it may suck from an educational perspective—it surely will not be your finest teaching moment—but it's not the end of the world either. Give the test, collect the bubble sheets—tra-la, tra-la—and keep moving.

Just because you have to give the tests doesn't mean you have to pretend to like them. You don't even have to think that standardized tests are valuable or worthwhile for you or for your students. Your part is administering the test, and that's the end of that particular story.

You can even, if you choose, try telling the truth about these tests to parents, to colleagues, and even to your students. Here's a truth-telling start: "Good morning, students. We'll be spending way too much time today, and for the next several weeks, preparing for high-stakes standardized tests, and yet the truth is that, even though the district requires these tests, and even though I'll be administering and you'll be taking these tests, the entire testing regime is a massive fraud."

OK, maybe you don't want to quite go there (or maybe a few of you, braver than the rest, will give it a shot) but no matter. You should at least know the truth about high-stakes standardized tests, and the truth is that big corporations profit from them—a major reason we're caught up in the testing regime—but these tests have nothing to do with real teaching or authentic learning.

> You should at least know the truth about high-stakes standardized tests. . . . They don't help teachers teach, they don't help parents know how their kids are doing, and they don't help students learn.

They don't help teachers teach, they don't help parents know how their kids are doing, and they don't help students learn. They fail even at their stated purpose: revealing the intelligence, talent, effort, or aptitude of students. The obsession with testing is lazy and wrong-headed from start to finish.

Testing has been a common cudgel in the hands of the powerful, a kind of modern and scientized eugenics device. But it has unleashed a forceful opposition as well—parents electing to have their children skip the tests, stay home, or sit in the auditorium during test time. Many families and entire communities have concluded that the tests are expensive and disruptive but have no authentic educational benefit, and many folks are becoming more sophisticated in analyzing the relative value of high-stakes standardized testing as well as the underpinnings of the entire obsession. One of the clearest objections is that the weight placed on certain standardized measures combined with the huge consequences—high stakes—makes gaming the system, that is, fudging and cheating, inevitable. After all, the testing competition is based on the "business model," and that approach includes maximizing profit regardless of consequences, dodging taxes, finding loopholes, hiding flaws, and hustling for the win. This explains in part why cheating scandals on student standardized tests are rampant across the land, and why authorities are barking up the wrong tree when they hire law enforcement to get to the bottom of things and secure the tests at all cost. Every week, somewhere in America, another scandal—and the root problem is not security, it's giving educators a hefty incentive to do the wrong thing.

The fraud is further revealed by "Goodhart's Law," named after the British economist Charles Goodhart, or the similar-but-different "Heisenberg Principle of Incentive Design," after the uncertainty principle at the heart of quantum physics: *A performance metric is only useful as a performance metric as long as it isn't used as a performance metric*, or, *When a measure becomes a target, it ceases to be a good measure.*

What that means is that if you want to build a "good high school," for example, and you announce that, say, 100% college attendance is the preferred indicator of whether you've built that desired "good high school," people will work frantically and single-mindedly toward that designated target, and it might even be achieved, but often to the detriment of the larger goal, that is, the school could still be terrible. One hundred percent of its graduates could indeed go to college (the performance metric) because every effort was bent in that single direction, but teachers and administrators glossed over an anemic curriculum, autocratic and rote teaching, a massive push-out rate, a sketchy list of what counts as "college," and astronomical college failure. Not good. The target became the goal, and the larger universe remained (and became more) miserable. You'll have to work hard to devise strategies and tactics that will help you resist and upend the toxic impacts of the testing madness on you and on your students. Telling kids the truth is only one step.

The whole modern testing regime distorts life for children and families and teachers. It reflects and reinforces the metaphor, language, and practices of education as a product to be bought and sold in the marketplace, as opposed to education as a universal human right and a site of intellectual freedom, moral reflection, courage, and ethical action.

The frenzy of testing is a big part of what can be thought of as a growing "audit culture," the seemingly endless requests for data, "value-added measures," quantifiable products, and one form after another to be filled out and filed by teachers. The audit culture changes the nature of intellectual inquiry and teaching into matters of consumption, intense competition, hierarchy, and privatized property; the result is the eclipse of the public and the destruction of the commons. While faculty may struggle against these demands here or there, what is often missed in these skirmishes is the deeper meaning and the wider contexts—a tightening death grip on the throat of education and an attack on the fundamental principles of schools for free people: critical thought, free inquiry, democratic community, and promoting the public good. Wreckage lies in the wake of the manufactured obsession with student and teacher accountability (coupled with zero accountability for foundations, corporations, hedge funds, bankers, and their government managers), the fateful weakening of intellectual independence, and the destruction of democratic life.

> The whole modern testing regime distorts life for children and families and teachers. It reflects and reinforces . . . education as a product to be bought and sold in the marketplace, as opposed to education as a universal human right and a site of intellectual freedom, moral reflection, courage, and ethical action.

When school is geared to the absorption of facts, learning becomes exclusively and exhaustively selfish, and there is no obvious social motive for it. When the measure of success is competitive, people are turned against one another and every difference becomes a score for somebody, and a wound for someone else. Getting ahead of others is a major goal, and mutual assistance, which can be so entirely natural in other human relations, is severely restricted or banned. A lot of "classroom management" problems are a direct result of the leaden structures of competition built into the heart of too many classrooms and schools.

Note as well that the testing machine can test only specific things, and those certain testable things then become glorified as the things-most-needful. The tail once again is wagging the dog. Albert Einstein famously noted that not everything that can be counted counts, and not everything that counts can be counted. Think, for example, about love, joy, justice, solidarity, beauty, kindness, compassion, commitment, peace, effort, interest, engagement, awareness, connectedness, happiness, sense of humor, relevance, honesty, self-confidence, respect for others, and . . . keep counting.

Twenty years ago in the United States the College Board, which owns the Scholastic Aptitude Test, acknowledged that the test had little to do with "aptitude" and dropped that word from its title, changing the name to the Scholastic *Achievement* Test. That wasn't quite right either, because the test can't say what's been achieved and so the name was changed again—it's now simply the SAT. The letters "SAT" stand for nothing more (nor less) than SAT. It makes some perverse sense that an exam named for itself measures only those skills needed for itself—the SAT.

The testing regime is hard to resist because it carries with it the insistent dogma of common sense, that is, a widely held and shared community understanding has it that the tests have a use that they in fact do not have. But since beliefs are not to be considered delusional if they're in keeping with accepted social norms, the focus on tests and testing is considered "sensible" and beyond debate. But remember: A good citizen of early Rome had the power to put his son to death; most Americans accepted for hundreds of years that owning another human being was a right; and an everyday American today believes that standardized tests tell us something worthwhile about children and teachers and teaching. It's the old story of the emperor who had no clothes—and we are in desperate need of the innocent child who can point out the obvious.

The Steinway Piano people proudly describe to the world that each one of their legendary baby grand pianos contains over 12,000 separate parts, explaining that no piano is exactly like any other, that each piano is unique, one of a kind. The wood of one tree is subtly different from the wood of another tree, and questions of age and humidity, growing conditions, light, and temperature all come into play. Moreover, constructing a Steinway is a labor of love and a creative if practical art—there is no assembly line and there are no robots that can get the job done properly. Each baby grand piano is the one of one, an astonishing 12,000 parts, fondly fabricated. Prospective buyers visit the showroom and typically sit at the keyboard sampling one and then another and another before deciding which one to purchase, and owners display genuine affection toward their own unique baby.

It's worth noting here that the number of neurons in a 3rd-grader's head is quite a bit more than 12,000—there are in fact upward of 100 billion neurons in that kid's brain. As teachers we know for sure that no child is exactly like any other—each is unique, one of a kind. Teaching and raising children is a labor of love and a creative if practical art—there is no assembly line and there are no bots that can get the job done properly. Each young person is the one of one, each with an astonishing 100 billion brain cells. Practicing and prospective teachers might want to keep that in mind as they develop authentic affection for the human beings before them, and a touch of awe toward the mighty profession they're a part of.

Oddly, people who think and care about Steinways are pretty certain that each is unique—and Steinway promotes that notion heavily—while the overlords who churn out policies about children and schools insist that kids aren't one of a kind, and in fact that there's a uniformity that can be discerned on a standardized test. They tend to talk about "the 3rd-grader" or "the 3rd-grade level" as if 3rd-graders were a thing—the same or similar—or as if the Platonic Ideal of "3rd-Grader" resides high above the clouds up there on Mount Olympus.

The fact is that learning does not take place in measurable pods, and constant testing does not contribute to enhanced performance. That way of thinking banishes conversation, exploration, and personalized approaches to teaching and learning. The classroom becomes dehumanized, and students are deprived of real opportunities to flex their intellectual muscles—let alone their social, cultural, or creative muscles.

Rather than exploring the knotty problem of what constitutes an education of value, or what we collectively think the wild diversity of educated persons ought to look like, or what kind of social and economic system would insist that the full development of each is the condition for the fullest development of all (and conversely, that the full development of all is the condition for the fullest development of each), the test-masters seem to want us all to bow low to the test and say, in effect, an educated person tests well, and we can line up educated folks, best to worst, on a neat and linear scale. And since the testing machine can test only specific, relatively narrow things, those constricted and testable things become glorified as the markers of value in education. This is an Alice in Wonderland world, everything upside down and everyone acting as if the Mad Hatter is completely sane.

You'll likely hear about "data-driven reform," and that's a fraud as well, and an adjunct to the test-and-punish idea. The testing regime is a continuing human catastrophe. We need a system that is "student-driven," "teacher- and community-built," and *data-informed*. To get there we need students, teachers, families, and community members who can name the system as it is, posit real alternatives, and rise up to fight for the schools we deserve and a society fit for all children—a place of peace and community, democracy and balance, joy and justice.

Enough!

Tell the truth—straightforward, plain, raw, sometimes difficult. That's step one.

: : :

Step two: Note that student assessment is a much larger universe than a single mass test—high-stakes standardized tests occupy only one corner of the assessment universe, even though they act a bit like black holes in space, sucking everything into their force fields, and then destroying them—and that authentic assessment of students in the hands of teachers matters enormously when you're creating an effective practice. So focus on authentic assessment, close to the students and in the service of making you a better teacher for each.

> You want to be clear in your own classroom and in your curriculum and teaching—as noted earlier—about the values, goals, and standards you're drawing on and deploying.

You want to be clear in your own classroom and in your curriculum and teaching—as noted earlier—about the values, goals, and standards you're drawing on and deploying. Yes, standards, meaning your principles and the models of excellence you're striving for, which is quite different from standardization, meaning a forced conformity to a standard determined by some external authority. You can have high standards for literacy, for example, or sophisticated levels of thinking and writing, without believing that everyone has to be on the same page in the same way on the same day. You can have high standards of group behavior without expecting everyone to act identically. People who watch baseball have in their minds an image and a standard of excellence when it comes to any position; take shortstop—several players come immediately to mind, including Javier Baez, Barry Larkin, Ozzie Smith, Cal Ripkin, Jr., Kris Davis, and Ernie Banks. Check their highlights and blow your mind. But also notice that not one of these players fields the position like any other. All brilliant, each different—standards, not standardization.

A core part of a teacher's daily work is assessment and evaluation, because knowing where each student is in terms of reading, for example, or math or history, matters in terms of calibrating the necessary support or the next challenge. Since each child is in constant motion, changing all the time, and since just when you've concluded that Javy, for instance, needs extra help with phonics, he's figured it out and moved on, and his new challenge is word recognition. You have to keep up.

Authentic assessment means looking closely and continuously at students' work and efforts in order to be a better, more relevant, and more finely tuned teacher. If students spend some class time working on a wide range of projects, performances, and portfolios—the Three P's—teachers will have more access to the real thinking of children and youth, and clearer opportunities to observe their minds in action.

Successful teachers have systems for collecting student work every day and every week, and student work often includes journal writing or visual representations, so that common interests as well as challenges can be identified. These teachers also take observational notes on two or three students every day, and over several days might realize that they have not focused on one or another child, and then deliberately correct for that omission. Some teachers read through student work folders every weekend to get a sense of each student's progress, challenges, obstacles, and priorities in anticipation of the coming week. Other teachers spend time organizing student work folders in order to have reflective conversations with kids, and serious, evidence-based conversations with parents during teacher/parent meetings.

I'm a proponent of portfolios for every class and every age. Here's a simple way to start: Begin with individual and/or group interviews in the first days of school focused on what students hope the class (or the year) will be like for them. What do you think 4th grade will be like? What are some things you'd most like to do this year? What were some roses and some thorns from school last year? Asking kids these kinds of questions is the start of evaluation and assessment for you, and creates a kind of anticipatory frame for them. It's a multifaceted start that takes nothing away from your ability to set and meet your own goals for class.

Tell the students that all year (or term) each of them will be working to create a unique portfolio representing a range of work experiences from the class, something to present in the final weeks of the school year. The portfolios can be as elaborate or as simple as you like, but the collection of objects that constitutes the portfolios should represent several opportunities for kids to shine and to be successful, being a summary of student efforts throughout the year, at the same time that they illustrate your goals and priorities for the class. Staying with the 4th-grade example, imagine that students knew from early on that each student-created portfolio would include an original piece of art, a short essay critiquing a piece of public art, a physical challenge that was set in the fall and completed by the spring, a self-selected "best" written story, a research project on a self-chosen topic, an original map of some important and interesting aspect of the community, an annotated list of her five favorite books from the year as well as what she plans to read over the summer, a description of some kind or generous act she carried out during the class, and on and on. Some teachers ask for grades and test scores to be nestled in the vast collection—not dominant, but present. Make a handout explaining each element, and perhaps create a big poster naming and illustrating the items you hope and expect the portfolios will ultimately contain.

Some teachers who use portfolios have each kid do an end-of-year presentation to the entire class, where work is shown, discussed, and evaluated. Others organize a committee made up, for example, of two peers, a parent or caregiver, a community member, and another teacher to examine and assess the portfolio as the student presents the work. In any case the classroom experience has become richer and fuller, deeper and truer, with the use of some form of portfolio.

CHAPTER : SEVEN

How Can I Create Some Productive Classroom Arrangements and a Bit of Positive Forward Motion with a Group of Energetic (or Disruptive!) Kids?

Are you concerned about issues of classroom discipline?

Do you worry about how you'll manage a large group of students in your own classroom—*all by yourself*?

Are your quiet moments sometimes haunted by images of feral children bouncing off the walls while you flee to the principal's office?

If so, welcome to the fevered anxieties of almost every new teacher anywhere in the country.

And if not, why not? You must know that there are more of them than there are of you, and that if students ever organized to overthrow the classroom regime you'd be knocked off the podium in seconds. You must have heard some of the well-rehearsed and oft-repeated horror stories.

Well, I have some good news and some bad news. First the bad news: It takes time to establish a productive and positive classroom atmosphere, tone, and feel, and the larger school may have a protocol in place that runs hard against the environment you aspire to build. There's a lot to take care of, a lot of challenges to meet and overcome. The students won't get there on the first day (or weeks) and neither will you. Be patient with yourself, and be patient with them. Work toward creating the right mood, step by deliberate step. The important thing to begin is to avoid the kind of missteps that will require dramatic revisions down the road. Think about where you want to be in a few months and go purposefully in that direction, inch by inch, row by row.

And the good news: You're not all by yourself, locked in combat with a much larger opposing force. Students are not your enemy, they are not your

> Students are not your enemy, they are not your adversaries, and you have to get that straight from the jump. . . . Your job is to mobilize the team, and set everyone in the right direction.

adversaries, and you have to get that straight from the jump. In fact, you're in the company of 25 or more potential allies—colleagues, co-teachers, and co-learners—all of whom have a stake in building a space of comfort, joy, productivity, and fairness. Your job is to mobilize the team, and set everyone in the right direction.

In order to do that I suggest you banish from your vocabulary three words that are typically deployed when we talk about classrooms: discipline, management, and control. *Discipline* is essentially the practice of "training people or animals to obey the rules, using punishment to correct disobedience." That seems like it ought to be the preserve of circus animals conditioned to perform mindlessly and obediently, or worse, it feels perilously close to the world of crime and punishment. *Management* is the "process of controlling things or people." Classroom management sounds like it belongs in the business school, not in a place devoted to the growth and learning of children. And *control* points toward the "power to direct other people's behavior." Each of these assumes a hierarchical order with a monopoly of power at the top. I want to think differently—power as shared and dispersed, not monopolized, and control as internal and self-regulated, not externally enforced.

The starting point for creating a functioning community of learners is to begin with the students themselves: What are their needs and concerns? How can we respond to those needs? What would make all students feel more comfortable, safe, and refreshed? This, rather than policy or tradition, should be your focus.

One teacher I know spent time early in the year in conversation with kids about safety and what it means to feel safe—physically, yes, but also emotionally. She asked them to take the throwaway cameras she'd provided and take pictures of where they felt safe. They came back with photos of bedrooms and kitchens, particular parks, a mother's lap, and all of it folded into an astonishing collage that filled a wall—and thus a deeper and broader conversation about the meaning of safety than she had thought possible when she began.

: : :

In his book *Discipline and Punish*, Michel Foucault analyzes the measures taken in the 17th century to combat the plague, a new threat that was lethal, invisible, and highly contagious. A new kind of disciplinary power was implemented, an approach that not only isolated a town or village in which an outbreak of the Black Death had occurred, but brought a group of people under intense scrutiny and segmentation, confining residents to their homes, placing sentinels at the corners of streets and intersections, and requiring regular review and registration of the position, condition, and identity of each individual under quarantine. To Foucault, the plague and the model of the quarantine led to the discovery of a new type of power, which he called "Discipline."

For Foucault a "mechanism of discipline" is any "enclosed, segmented space, observed at every point, in which the individuals are inserted in a fixed place, in which the slightest movements are supervised, in which all events are recorded, in which uninterrupted links exist between the center and periphery." Sounds eerily like a lot of schools.

The architectural expression of this disciplinary power is Jeremy Bentham's "Panopticon," a model prison built upon a simple concept with echoing and accelerating implications: a tower surrounded by a ring of cells. A supervising guard stands in the central tower; he can observe each of the prisoners, but they can neither see him nor one another; prisoners never know when or how they're being observed, but recognize at all times their own visibility and vulnerability: "Hence the major effect of the Panopticon: to induce in the inmate a state of conscious and permanent visibility that assures the automatic functioning of power." Again, all too recognizable as the standard of power in the modern world, and increasingly familiar in contemporary schools.

What Foucault calls "The swarming of disciplinary mechanisms" ensures that disciplinary powers "have a certain tendency to become de-institutionalized, to emerge from the closed fortresses in which they once functioned and to circulate in a 'free' state." In other words, what begins as an effort to regulate and control certain marginal or dangerous segments of the population—victims of the plague, prisoners, the insane—becomes a technology used to normalize the population as a whole, adopted by all institutions with any interest whatsoever in power and authority. "Is it surprising," asks Foucault rhetorically, "that prisons resemble factories, schools, barracks, hospitals, which all resemble prisons?" No, it's not.

One dreadful result is that schools sink more and more of their budgets into "security" while dramatically narrowing the curriculum, eliminating programs in sports, music, the arts, and more. School architecture is redesigned with an emphasis on surveillance. Some schools have taken the Panopticon to an odious extreme, designing buildings so that one person, presumably the school principal, can stand in his or her office and have an unobstructed view of the entire facility. The message: I can see you.

The venetian blinds that Bentham imagined in the central tower of his Panopticon to hide the guard from the prisoners in the outside ring have been replaced by the ubiquitous black globes covering security cameras that can be wired into local police stations, projecting the unobstructed gaze of state power directly into the school hallways or even the classroom. Some schools have begun more Orwellian projects, including pilot programs in Radio Frequency Identification (RFID), which puts electronic tags on student IDs in order to trace students' movements on a central computerized map. Other schools use GPS technology to shadow bus fleets, metal detectors and bomb-sniffing dogs at entryways, and fingerprint readers and biometric hand scanners to track attendance and library withdrawals.

In such an environment, teachers can easily and routinely become instruments of disciplinary surveillance—tracking, labeling, observing, categorizing, and disciplining students. We do it—policing student work for signs of potential violence, extracting feelings and motives from creative expressions and comparing these motives against a battery of normalized prescriptions in our heads—and we read or hear stories of the more extreme examples: teachers who report students to the police or even to the Secret Service for perceived violent threats gleaned from school journals, creative writing, or homework assignments.

On the other hand, we teachers are often ourselves the objects of disciplinary surveillance: the cameras, background checks, urine tests, and "professional evaluation" systems that categorize, fix, and supervise us in our everyday activities. There are as well the disciplinary procedures of standardized curricula and random checks by education officials who can show up in our classrooms at any time and physically check students' workbooks to make sure we've reached the required page for a specified date. Such surveillance intervenes in the teacher-student relationship, and in the pedagogical process itself.

:   :   :

In place of—and in opposition to—all of this discipline, management, and control, I want to create, in effect, an entire curriculum called "Learning to Live Together" that lives simultaneously and alongside everything else we do in class. Learning to Live Together can be an explicitly discussed and noted standard, and it can be, as well, an implicitly assumed expectation, a normal part of everything else we do in class. It's intended to be a *lived* curriculum, sometimes calling attention to itself on occasion, but most often merely a norm, an unexceptional touchstone, an internalized guideline.

Learning to Live Together is where the reality of being a singular and unique individual—the one-of-one—and being one person in a much larger group—simply one of the many—comes to life in practice. We don't have a rulebook or a set of potential crimes and punishments, but we do have an overarching ethic: Respect yourself and respect one another; respect the world and respect the work. Opportunities for teachable moments will erupt every day—conflict and resolution—and those may become the unrehearsed yet finest moments of your teaching life, as well as important opportunities for students to experience authentic learning and deeper understanding.

Of course there will be moments when you will have to curb a particular behavior or action of this or that specific student, either in that student's best interest or in the interest of the larger community. But a Learning to Live Together approach asks that you accompany any reprimand or direct instruction—implicitly or explicitly—with a simple phrase: *because I love you.* Don't run in the street, *because I love you.* Stop fighting, *because I love you.* You have to take a short time out, *because I love you.* We're learning to live together in this class (and in this world), and that means we have to figure out how to cooperate, compromise, and give and take sometimes. And when you as the teacher (older, more experienced) have to intervene in order to help everyone figure out the complex reality of living together, be sure that all of your students get the message—that they hear it, experience it, understand it: *because I love you.*

> Opportunities for teachable moments will erupt every day—conflict and resolution—and those may become the unrehearsed yet finest moments of your teaching life, as well as important opportunities for students to experience authentic learning and deeper understanding.

One teacher I know has a large poster taped on the back wall with the heading in bold caps: **LEARNING TO LIVE TOGETHER.** She has three points listed beneath that heading: (1) We are a community of learners; (2)

We respect ourselves and one another; (3) We respect the work, our class-room, our school, our community, and our shared world. There are pencils and a stack of sticky-notes at a small table nearby, and students write out their thinking and ideas about how these points are (or are not) being en-acted in class, and then attach them to the large poster. These notes and comments lead to regular dialogue and discussion about how everyone can do a better job.

This is intended to stand in sharp contrast to the obsession with obedi-ence, standardization, conformity, and control that characterizes too many classrooms—enforced with a vengeance in schools attended by the descen-dants of enslaved people, immigrant children from poor countries, and First Nations youth. Knowing and accepting one's place on the grand pyr-amid of winners and losers becomes the core lesson. These schools devel-op elaborate schemes for managing the unruly mob, and they turn on the familiar technologies of constraint—ID cards, transparent backpacks, uni-form dress codes, cameras, armed guards, metal detectors, random search-es. The knotted system of rules, the exhaustive machinery of schedules and surveillance, the Panopticon-like architecture, the laborious programs of regulating, indoctrinating, inspecting, disciplining, censuring, correcting, counting, appraising, assessing and judging, testing and grading—all of it makes these "schools" institutions of punishment rather than sites of en-lightenment and liberation. They have become places to recover from rath-er than experiences to carry forward.

: : :

When a school functions as a Panopticon the students become its little political prisoners—the most wide-awake of them know it. Compelled by the state to attend, handed a schedule, a uniform, and a rulebook, sent to a specific designated space of cellblocks, monitored constantly and controlled relentlessly—Pledge of Allegiance: 9:00; No talking; Bathroom break: 10:15–10:20; No eating in the classroom; Lunch: 11:45–12:05; Boys and girls form separate lines; Dismissal bell: 3:10; No running in the hallways. On and on and on, the whole catalogue of coercion under forced confinement—every young body the object of domination and control.

The "Uniform Discipline Code" of the Chicago Public Schools, a case in point, grows, it seems, several pages a year. Its putative goal is "To pro-mote desirable student conduct and behavior," its approach to "Codify the penalties that shall be applicable system-wide, yet retain administrative flexibility in their application"—a task that could keep a battery of Board of Education lawyers busy for months, with a neat loophole large enough for a yellow school bus full of gangbangers to drive through.

The book has preliminary chapters on responsibilities and rights for students, parents, teachers, and principals. Students and teachers are instructed, for example, to "Observe basic standards of cleanliness, modesty, and good grooming," while principals, interestingly, have no comparable responsibility according to the book. Perhaps it's assumed that principals, but not teachers, have figured out how to keep and look clean. Maybe that's how they got to be principals.

Student responsibilities go on and on: "Be honest and courteous," "Have pride in your school," "Improve your performance upon notice of unsatisfactory progress"—21 bullet points in all. Parents have only 12 points, the first of which speaks volumes about expectations: "Present to school officials your case/cause in a calm, reasoned manner." One can feel the gulf, the wall, the antagonism. Teachers are, of course, to "Devote school hours exclusively to official duties"—is this necessary?—and principals to "Notify the Chicago Police Department as necessary." Really?

"Student Misconduct" is divided into six neat groupings: Group 1 is "*inappropriate* student behaviors" such as "Running and/or making excessive noise in the hall or building," or "Being improperly dressed," all of which result in conferences. Group 2 is *disruptive*, Group 3 *seriously disruptive*, Group 4 *very seriously disruptive*, and Group 5 *most seriously disruptive* behavior, each with its accompanying and escalating sanctions and punishments. Group 6 consists of "Acts of misconduct [that] include illegal student behaviors that not only *most seriously disrupt* the orderly educational process . . . but also mandate . . . disciplinary action" from 10-day suspensions to expulsions.

Group 2 behaviors include "Posting or distributing unauthorized or other written materials on school grounds"; Group 3, "Gambling" and "Forgery"; Group 4, "Extortion," "Assault," and "Disorderly conduct"; Group 5, "Aggravated assault," "Gang activity, including repeated overt displays of gang affiliation." Group 6 behaviors are acts like "Arson," "Bomb threats," "Murder," "Kidnapping," and "Sex violations." Kidnapping? Murder?

The book ends with a convenient 6-page glossary written with the help of an indecipherable legal dictionary: "Indecent proposition—An unsolicited sexual proposal"; "Look-alike substance—Any substance which by appearance, representation, or manner of distribution would lead a reasonable person to believe that the substance is an illegal drug"; "Disorderly conduct—an act done in an unreasonable manner so as to alarm or disturb others and which provokes a breach of the peace."

Of course, the growing heft of the book speaks only to the failure of officials to really grasp the adolescent and misbehaving imagination, which is both expansive and limitless—it knows no bounds. General commandments like "be courteous" and "dress properly" are both obvious and hopelessly vague; more specific demands—"No running," "No bullying," "No display of gang affiliation" are also vague—thank goodness for that cleverly retained "administrative flexibility." But the grown-ups want to appear serious, and, as is often the case, they don't quite get it: The more crimes you catalog, the more ideas you generate; the more misdemeanors you name, the more creative sins heave into view.

The little prison administrators expect neither uniform compliance nor automatic submission from every inmate, hence the elaborate mechanisms for uprooting deviance, for hammering each one into a model prisoner—obedient, compliant, conforming.

Schools don't exist outside of history, of course, or culture: They are, rather, at the heart of each. As both mirror and window, schools show us what we value. Authoritarian societies are served by authoritarian schools, just as free schools support free societies. If you know that a given society is fascist—Germany in the 1930s, say—certain classroom characteristics are entirely predictable: The tone will be authoritative, the discipline will be harsh, the pedagogy domineering, the curriculum manipulative. Conversely, if you visit a school and see those same qualities, you can predict that the larger society is hierarchical and imperious, even if it wraps itself in high and noble phrases: the Fatherland or Homeland, Patriotism, Freedom. This doesn't mean that authoritarian schools with their propagandistic curriculum, manipulative relationships, and harsh, coercive methods necessarily produce people without skills— Nazi Germany, medieval Saudi Arabia, and apartheid South Africa all turned out brilliant doctors and scientists, artists and athletes.

> Schools don't exist outside of history, of course, or culture: They are, rather, at the heart of each.

:   :   :

From the perspective of a humane or democratic society, the authoritarian approach is always backward—it subverts the participatory spirit of democratic living, it disrupts community, it aims to destroy independent and free thought, and it undermines critical reasoning. Democracy demands active, thinking human beings, and education is designed to empower and to enable that goal. Furthermore, a vital democracy requires participation, some tolerance and acceptance of

> Democracy demands active, thinking human beings, and education is designed to empower and to enable that goal.

difference, some independent thought, a spirit of mutuality—in other words, Learning to Live Together.

"I shall create!" a juvenile delinquent cries out in Gwendolyn Brooks's poem "Boy Breaking Glass," and the words, coming from the mouth of this imagined "bad boy," land with particular power and poignancy. "If not a note, a hole," he continues, "If not an overture, a desecration." No matter what you've been told, Brooks cautions, and no matter what the pundits and talking heads have insistently professed, never doubt for a moment the urgent intent of even the most marginalized and outcast youth among us: *I shall create.*

It's up to us—teachers, parents, community members—to answer that heartfelt cry, that elemental human aspiration. This means seeing these outcasts as whole and dynamic human beings through the blizzard of stereotypes that engulf them, hearing their authentic voices above the steady roar of commentary about them. For classroom teachers it means opening the creative vent, encouraging the creation of notes and overtures, so that the destructive vent atrophies from lack of use.

∴ ∴ ∴

Each of us is a distinct and singular individual, the one-and-only or the one-of-one, like no other; each merely one of the many, a small part of the group, just like all others. Try to live inside that contradiction—each is like no other, each is like some others, each is like all others—and to hold those opposing ideas in mind as we move forward, learning to live together. Here's another instance:

"Freedom Now!" was the watchword of the Black Freedom Movement 50 years ago, and the battle cry of every anticolonial and anti-imperialist liberation struggle throughout the world in the second half of the 20th century. Those movements embraced demands for individual liberties— the right to vote, to access public goods and resources, to live and eat and sit and drink water where one wished—but always within a larger vision of collective freedom, freedom for a community and for an entire people.

Similarly, "women's liberation" and "gay liberation" movements brought a self-identified "public" into being through the process of fighting oppression, discrimination, ill treatment, or abuse that was faced by people on the basis of their membership in a particular group or community. Freedom and liberation meant resistance to exploitation and oppression, the possibility of becoming more fully realized human beings with agency and the social power to participate without restriction. We demanded freedom for the group, freedom for *us,* a collection of many, many me's.

But "freedom" can easily come to mean simply free choice today, personal freedom, freedom not for a collective *we,* but freedom for an individual *me.* The right to do your own thing and the community be damned is a far cry from the social meaning of freedom to those various liberation movements. "Freedom" is today heralded by leaders of the gig economy and the San Francisco Bay Area's new libertarian tech culture as well as by members of the ultraright Freedom Caucus in the U.S. House of Representatives—"freedom" to extract profits through capitalist markets unfettered by public input or government regulation.

In Boots Riley's dazzling film *Sorry to Bother You,* a corporation called "Worry Free" promises customers free food and free housing, freedom from the stress of looking for a job and freedom from paying your annoying bills. Sounds great, right? But all that freedom comes with a catch: You have to sign a lifetime work contract. TV ads for "Worry Free" feature happy—White—families smiling their carefree smiles as they walk hand-in-hand toward their promised worry-free future. Of course "Worry Free" is modern-day slavery wearing the mask of freedom, but it takes a minute to catch on because it's so cleverly marketed to appeal to those of us who are bathed in the blood of our pervasive consumer culture. It's an important if bitter reminder that "freedom" was not only the goal of the abolitionists fighting to free the enslaved workers, but also the motto of the Confederacy—organized traitors and terrorists willing to burn down the house in order to preserve a single "freedom": their freedom to own other human beings.

: : :

Teachers can create classrooms where students with a range of backgrounds, perspectives, experiences, and beliefs can learn from one another even as they learn to live with one another. A pedagogy of dialogue—beginning with a question, and then asking the next question, and then the next—is the basic teaching gesture in and for a free and democratic society. Learning the fine art of speaking with the possibility of being heard, and listening with the possibility of being changed, is a practical contribution to finding one's way in a wildly diverse democracy. This is what Learning to Live Together is all about.

> Teachers can create classrooms where students with a range of backgrounds, perspectives, experiences, and beliefs can learn from one another even as they learn to live with one another. A pedagogy of dialogue—beginning with a question, and then asking the next question . . .

And while Learning to Live Together is a good addition to any classroom—in preschool it's a way to resolve conflicts and talk about no fighting/no biting; in high school no shaming/no bullying; and in a graduate school seminar no domineering/no silencing—it's also something to be taken seriously in every relationship, every social setting, throughout your life.

CHAPTER : EIGHT

How Do I Work with Parents
(and with Colleagues/Administrators)?

My partner and I dreaded the approaching parent/teacher conference—and with good reason.

We'd moved from New York to Chicago a few months earlier, and our three young sons had been attending a new school, making new friends, facing unaccustomed routines and new demands for just four short weeks. We'd adopted our youngest son when he was 14 months old; now in the 2nd grade, he was what was euphemistically called a "challenging child." In his case that meant that he had difficulty making friends and sometimes initiated angry confrontations with other children, and that his temper tantrums could spiral out of control and rage on for hours (or even days). Specialists and shrinks went on and on: self-destructive behaviors; poor impulse control; little interest in group activities; long periods of low energy; general lack of focus. Furthermore, he couldn't read. We were sure that the teacher would tick off the whole list in an aggrieved tone of voice, and would likely document the case with some specifically appalling news about his behavior in class—and I was absolutely determined to stick up for our son at any cost and at every turn. We were not looking forward to this parent/teacher conference, obviously, and we inched toward it with anxiety and a growing sense of foreboding.

After we'd exchanged greetings with the teacher and had taken our seats around a table, the young teacher surprised us with this: "You know your son much, much better than I will ever know him; what can you tell me that will help me be a better teacher for him?"

I was prepared for a struggle, but all the fight suddenly disappeared, and combat no longer seemed remotely reasonable. I mumbled something about our son's temper, and I could almost feel the teacher saying, "No shit," but he didn't say it. He listened attentively and asked smart questions, and before long we were sharing our deepest fears and our fondest hopes, and the three of us were becoming cooperating members of the same team, all of us wanting the best outcomes for our kid.

He told us at some point that he'd discovered in these few weeks that if he gave our son real work to do, a classroom task that mattered, he would stay at it relentlessly until he'd completed it. "He loves to do clean-up, and if I ask him, for example, to take all the books and supplies off the shelves, wash and dry them, and then put everything back, he can stay with that task for a long time." He added that when things like that can be organized, our son "comes into clearer focus" for the other students, for the teacher, "but most important, for himself." He's no longer exclusively the kid with monstrous tantrums; he's now the kid with tantrums who does a great job cleaning the shelves. The difference, believe me, is monumental.

In that first meeting the teacher accomplished something extraordinary—something that you can aspire to with every parent of every student you teach. He deflected what might have been a difficult or antagonistic encounter, and he built a purposeful partnership with us. He did it in part with that brilliant opening question, which took us off the defensive and invited us to begin to trust him and to talk more openly, and in part with the story of the bookshelves, which indicated to us that he already knew our son pretty well, and that he had developed by now a hopeful perspective on him as a person and as a learner.

: : :

> Parents and caregivers, far from being your antagonists, are potentially your second-greatest allies and partners, right next to the students themselves.

The thought of dealing with parents gives many teachers the chills—and not just new teachers—but it shouldn't. Parents and caregivers, far from being your antagonists, are potentially your second-greatest allies and partners, right next to the students themselves. Parents are your students' first teachers, and as such they're your colleagues and co-teachers (or perhaps, from their perspective, you're their temporary co-madre or co-padre) with their own unique experiences and expertise. You have a lot in common: You both want to see these children and youth grow into capable and smart adults; you both want them to become good and moral members of their larger communities; you both want them to be able to do productive work; you both want them to be able to love and be loved in return. That's a lot of agreement to build on.

Unfortunately, the tension between parents and teachers is stubborn—go to any teachers' lunchroom and you'll hear people talking trash about parents; go to any local laundry or playground and listen to people complain about teachers. Sarah Lawrence Lightfoot wrote a book about this conflict called *Worlds Apart*, and one chapter has the fraught title, "Teachers and Mothers: The Other Woman." Can it really be that bad, a tooth-and-nail fight filled with jealousy, anger, and bad faith? It can be that bad, but it's not preordained. The relationship doesn't have to be bad at all, and you can be the one to interrupt and untangle that old, sterile contradiction; shine a light into the darkness; and construct something productive and mutually advantageous in its place—and while everyone will win, the main beneficiaries will be the children.

And like the kids every parent is dynamic, on the move, in the mix, and a three-dimensional human being as well, just like you—the one-of-one, and one of the many. Take it on faith. They too have hearts and minds, spirits and souls, experiences and perspectives, hopes and histories, passions and preferences, aspirations and dreams—the point of connection for the relationship you need to build is a focus on the child. Period. You don't have to be close or in agreement or sympathetic on every level; you simply have to find a way to connect around your shared concern for this specific child, and this one and this one.

And just like the kids, no parent should be glibly stereotyped by you: "uncooperative," "meddling," "high-strung," "pushy," "thinks his kid is a princess." Whatever presenting performances or behaviors led you to that label, you must know that these simple summaries can't possibly hold up in every context. Again, look more deeply, or look more generously: "Thinks his kid is a princess" could surely be annoying, but better than being indifferent or cruel to his daughter. The parents have to be visible enough, in focus enough, for you to understand a bit more clearly their motives, needs, hopes, and desires. You don't have to be best friends with any parent, but you do need to be able to communicate clearly and over time about his or her child.

You've heard the well-worn phrase, "All children can learn." It's true, of course, and self-evident, and it's been made into a cliché for well-intentioned educators. I might modify it a little: "All kids are learning all the time—but not necessarily what you want them to learn." But there's a larger point: If all kids can learn—agreed—at what point do we say, "OK, that's it, she just turned 18 (21? 30?) and it's over; she can't learn anything anymore. Forget about it. Remember: All children can learn, but she's not a child." Clearly that's nonsense. You're still learning, and other adults you know are also learning all the time. We're not static or stuck. Ask any parent and you'll find that they're having new insights and discoveries about parenting every step along the way. So here's a kindred slogan: "All parents can learn!" Your task is to create the space where you and your students' parents can learn together and from one another.

: : :

If your goal is authentic communication and co-learning, traditional approaches to parent/teacher relationships are anemic at best, and often doomed from the start. Top-down or one-directional interactions hardly count as relationships at all. So if you plan to wait for parents to contact you or if you reach out to them only when their child is having some difficulty or problem, you're not building a useful relationship. If you talk with them only when you need their assistance—asking them to volunteer on a class trip or telling them to provide more homework support—you are not creating the conditions for real exchange. You have to try something new.

You should find ways to reach out regularly and routinely—and from the start—in the belief that they are equal stakeholders in creating a vibrant and successful classroom. Some teachers, like Mr. Rob, do a home visit before school begins. Others make a point of calling home every week or two, just to check in and catch up. Some teachers send a one-page newsletter home every Friday—"This Week in Room 204." And others have a book on a table near the front door called "Class Notes" where they can write observations and ideas that parents can read at drop-off or pick-up, and where parents can share news or thoughts that they think the teacher ought to know. I know a teacher who organizes a family picnic in the fall and another in the spring. I know another teacher who has a monthly book club with any parents who are interested in reading and discussing novels together.

I know an elementary school that has a policy against homework. It's true. These educators argue that most homework is in reality schoolwork done at home, creating anxiety and stress in the family, and that schoolwork should be done in school, period. They add that every student should spend a screen-free hour reading outside of school every day, and that each should play a board game with a family member. Home work.

Parent conferences might mimic the one described above, a time of listening before talking, sharing student experiences and student work. If your school organizes a parents' night (and if it doesn't, organize one on your own), use the time for some hands-on learning: Invite parents to spend a little time building with blocks, or working at the easels, or playing board games, or accessing the reading lab or composition corner; your conversation about curriculum and instruction, child development and the complexity of learning, will have much more sizzle and bite after they've dug into your learning environment. You might also share with them your process when it comes to curriculum development, and solicit their thoughts and ideas. Listen to their issues and concerns. This is all in the interest of real collaboration toward building a deep and long-term relationship. And it acknowledges something too often ignored or lost: Working with parents is a necessary and potentially crucial part of your job.

: : :

Working with colleagues and administrators should be guided by the same ethos: Each of them is a three-dimensional being as well; each of them is on a journey through life that deserves your patience and empathy and respect. Resist the human tendency to sum folks up and make hard and fast judgments. Look more deeply. Note that we are all (you and I included) hopelessly fragile and flawed, limited all of the time and wrong much of the time. Search for common ground.

One gesture you might make that could help to create a more positive culture in the school even as it provides a unique horizontal staff development experience for yourself would be to organize with a few other teachers a Teacher Talk group at your school. Here's how it works: Get 3–7 teachers to

> Note that we are all (you and I included) hopelessly fragile and flawed, limited all of the time and wrong much of the time. Search for common ground.

commit to meeting once a week or once every other week for 40 minutes (minimum) in one of their classrooms, a different room every meeting. You could meet after school, before school, or during a common prep period if that can be organized. The teachers don't have to be "like-minded" or in full agreement; they only have to be interested in and committed to a teacher-centered and teacher-led conversation about the content and conduct of teaching and learning.

This is a no-whine zone, so 60 seconds of complaint time is the limit—I get it: Teachers do have a lot to complain about, too many kids, for example, too little time, and too few resources. But the culture of whining can quickly become too much as it goes round and round and begins to swallow its own tail. So acknowledge it, and then limit it or stop it. Move on.

The meeting officially begins with the host teacher showing the group around the environment for learning for 10 minutes, explaining to the other teachers the thinking that went into each space and every choice. The group then takes 10 minutes to talk back to the host teacher with suggestions, ideas, possibilities. Next the host teacher takes 10 minutes to present a portrait of a student through that student's work, and again the group responds for 10 minutes with thoughts, connections, recommendations. Forty minutes and done. Next week a different classroom, a different host, but the same rhythm to the discussion.

Teacher Talk is an antidote to cynicism and despair; it's a practical response to the winter doldrums and the potential of experiencing terminal burnout. It offers a forum to focus with your peers on the content and the practice of the work, and a regular venue to address the inevitable challenges and crises classroom teachers face.

The magic of Teacher Talk is that it unlocks the wisdom in the room, and allows teachers to face one another in genuine partnership and cooperation. I think schools should have a complete moratorium on spending any money at all on staff development offered by outside vendors, entrepreneurs, or corporations. Horizontal staff development is free, and more powerful and compelling for all involved.

CHAPTER : NINE

How Should I Develop My Own Unique Teaching Signature?

Mr. Rob teaches 4th grade, and while I've never actually seen him teach, I get weekly reports of classroom life from a 10-year-old named Luz who tells me, "I love Mr. Rob." I love him too, and here's why:

According to my eyewitness Mr. Rob's class is always filled with interesting challenges and projects. On one wall is a large portrait of Beyoncé, and on another he's designed a captivating collage of pictures of himself with each student from when he did home visits in the few days before the school year began. "He's a strict guy," Luz says, "but not cold or mean." I ask her to say more about that, and she adds, "Well, he really cares a lot about smooth transitions, going from one thing to another, and he has this little mantra he always repeats—'quickly, quietly, and under control.'"

When I asked her to describe Mr. Rob's teaching signature, Luz said, "Huh?" You know, I continued, the theme of his class, the thing that makes him special and unique, different from all the other teachers. What does he stand for as a teacher? "Oh," she said without missing a beat. "Curiosity."

That's a pretty cool teaching signature on the face of it, right?

But Luz isn't done, and so she elaborates: "Every kid has a Wonder Book in their desk where they can record questions that come up in class or at home. They can get filled

> What does he stand for as a teacher? "Oh," she said without missing a beat. "Curiosity."

up pretty fast with everyone asking and sharing questions. And if you ask Mr. Rob a question, he immediately tells you to write that in your Wonder Book. He almost never answers questions directly, but says things like, 'Think about it' or 'Let it marinate.' He's big on hypothesizing [I know—precocious little 10-year-old, right?], and he says, 'No Googling' and 'No instant gratification.'" The kids sometimes call him the Curious Cat.

He's constantly playing what he calls the Question Game with the kids—every question he's asked is answered by a question from him rather than an immediate (and, he would say, partial or superficial) answer. He wants to keep the conversation open, to develop curious dispositions of mind, and to illustrate how complex and multifaceted every little thing actually is. He wants kids to pursue questions to the outer limits. So Luz was reading a story one day and asked him, What's the life expectancy of a wild turkey, and he said, Why do turkeys have wattles? She responded, Can wild turkeys fly? He asked, What's their natural habitat? She said, Why are they called turkeys anyway? And so it went—no lazy answers or quick judgments, no instant gratification or easy dogma—just the next question, and then the next question after that.

Each day begins with Mr. Rob greeting kids at the door and giving handshakes or hugs or high fives—as each prefers. He lets the students fill their water bottles (he gave each one a small water bottle with their name painted on it with red fingernail polish when he did home visits, thereby winning them over instantly!), get organized at their desks, and read quietly for a few minutes before calling them to a large circular rug for morning meeting.

There's always a lot to discuss: There's the "word of the day" (ingenuity, garish, methodical—I'm not kidding!), which each student will try to use in a sentence in the course of the day; there's looking back to yesterday and forward to plans for the coming day and beyond; and invariably there's a little time every morning to talk about the progress of their Wonder Circles, small groups that work together to investigate a question or topic for 2 or 3 weeks, which will culminate in a presentation to the class. One time there were Wonder Circles of four or five students looking at Fossil Fuel, Land Fill, Steel Production, and Coal Mining. Luz's group was investigating Green Energy, and the group put on a culminating skit with Luz playing Hydropower.

Mr. Rob's musical tastes are eclectic; he often has jazz or classic rock playing softly in the background while students work. But occasionally he brings a song front and center in morning meeting. Luz remembers one day when they all listened to Tracy Chapman's "Why?" Mr. Rob had printed out the lyrics, which included the kinds of questions he savored: "Why do babies starve when there's enough food to feed the world?" "Why when there's so many of us are there people still alone?"

He occasionally calls for Mindful Moments, and kids assume their Mindful Body positions: Sit up straight, quiet and with eyes closed, hands down. He might say, "We'll do the pink bubble practice," and everyone puts their worries in an imagined pink bubble and then visualizes the bubble rising to the ceiling and bursting—worries gone for now!

Mr. Rob has a large whiteboard with question starters, and kids add their own throughout the year. Question starters are things like, If I put Blank and Blank together I'd get Blank, or Do Blank always like to Blank? On another poster Mr. Rob writes out his Question of the Week: How can you enhance your role as a citizen? What's the difference between an issue and a problem? If you could bestow three qualities on every student in this class, what would they be? Why?

So when Luz—and I imagine other students as well—thinks of Mr. Rob, the unique and unforgettable quality that jumps to mind is curiosity. No wonder she loves him—curiosity won her over.

: : :

Thinking about what your teaching signature might be is a way to transcend the hard, complex work of teaching—and, yes, to repeat, teaching is really hard work, and teaching is excruciatingly complex. So bringing your own personal passions, enthusiasms, interests, hobbies, or amusements into the classroom is a vital way to have some of the joy of your one cherished life woven into the everyday reality of your classroom. Perhaps you like basketball or limericks or baking pies or spoken-word poetry or flying kites or mysteries or puns or gardening or cultivating mushrooms or yoga or crossword puzzles or piano or whatever. Don't park your passions at the schoolhouse door; invite them in, and make a bit of space for them to stretch out and breathe.

I have a teacher friend who is a quilter and a weaver—every student in her class builds a little wooden lap loom early in the year, and each learns in the course of the year to use, as well, a backstrap loom and the larger Navaho frame loom that dominates the back table. Over several months they collectively construct a patchwork quilt representing the experiences and events of their school year together.

Another friend is a storyteller who has taken countless classes and workshops, practiced telling stories to random groups of kids on Saturday mornings at the Hans Christian Andersen statue in Central Park, and is part of the National Storytelling Network and the National Association of Black Storytellers. Stories are part of everything that goes on in her classroom, from the beginning to the end of each day. Other things are going on as well, of course, but she is a brilliant narrator herself, and learning to write and tell a good story to the class is something every student does multiple times during the school year. Every one in the school refers to her as the Story Woman, and anyone who's ever been in her class would tell you unhesitatingly that her teaching signature is storytelling.

: : :

What are some of the things that mark you as the unique and singular person that you are? How could some of those interests or enthusiasms find an appropriate and meaningful place in your classroom?

You may not be the Story Woman or the Weaver or the Curious Cat, so who will you be? What are some of the things that mark you as the unique and singular person that you are? How could some of those interests or enthusiasms find an appropriate and meaningful place in your classroom?

Ms. Stacey's room is decorated with her own original oil paintings of birds. She's been a birder her whole life, and she studied painting in high school and college. In her vast library (she's been teaching for 14 years) are dozens of bird books: *The Hummingbird Book, The Owls Coloring Book, Birds of Prey, Birds of the Amazon*, and more. She has a pet parrot named Pat who lives in the room, too. On the art table are supplies that can be used to build birdhouses or puppets during Free Choice Time. Ms. Stacey is the Bird Person.

Ms. Vida has a keyboard at the front of her room, and a guitar perpetually on her back or at her side. She calls the class to the carpet with a few chords, and signals transitions and the end of the school day with song. She calls her subject-area teaching "workshops"—"math workshop," "science workshop," "English workshop"—and during "composition workshop" she plays piano, and calls the practice "Notes for Notes." Her students sing together and clap softly as they walk the hallways to lunch or gym, defying the "silence" rule of the larger school, mostly tolerated because it's a lovely alternative to complete quiet, and, well, it's just Ms. Vida's peculiarity—and we can all learn to make some allowances for gentle eccentricities.

Take some time to think about what your teaching signature might be. . . . Unearth it; organize it; transport it to the classroom. Bring in your expertise as well as your bliss.

Take some time to think about what your teaching signature might be. Think about what you have in your home or your regular routine or your leisure time that lights you up. Unearth it; organize it; transport it to the classroom. Bring in your expertise as well as your bliss. What the kids will take away from your class is not the birding or the mushroom farming necessarily (some might!), but the sense of excitement and purposefulness and awe and amazement to be found in our marvelous shared world—and you showed them how that looks and feels.

CHAPTER : TEN

What Commitments Should I Bring with Me into the Classroom?

Here's Walt Whitman, in one of his many propulsive prefaces to *Leaves of Grass*:

> This is what you shall do:
>
> Love the earth and sun and the animals, despise riches, give alms to everyone that asks, stand up for the stupid and crazy, devote your income and labor to others, hate tyrants, argue not concerning God, have patience and indulgence toward the people, take off your hat to nothing known or unknown or to any man or number of men, go freely with powerful uneducated persons and with the young and with the mothers of families, re-examine all you have been told at school or church or in any book, dismiss whatever insults your own soul, and your very flesh shall be a great poem and have the richest fluency not only in its words but in the silent lines of its lips and face and between the lashes of your eyes and in every motion and joint of your body . . .

Nice start, Walt. That's a list to carry along in your backpack, a list to tape to your wall. It's written to poets, but it stands as pretty great advice for free teachers, too.

There's so much in those few lines, but I especially embrace this: *dismiss whatever insults your own soul.*

As a teacher I take that to mean don't teach against your conscience—which can be a serious and ongoing challenge in some institutions—and always try to live your teaching life in a way that won't make a mockery of your teaching values. As Mr. Rob might say, marinate on that for a bit.

My brother, a legendary California high school teacher, often said, "I may be an agent of the system or of the state for several hours a day, but I'm

> You should name the
> various commitments
> you're bringing with you into
> teaching, spell them out as
> best you can now so that
> you have a handy list to post
> on the bathroom mirror,
> something to consult each
> morning. . . . Make it simple
> and true—these are your
> fundamental commitments
> to yourself and to your
> students.

a free agent the rest of the time, and I squeeze every drop of life and light out of each moment of freedom—that's where I'm the teacher I truly want to be," and that's where his commitments come to life. We may perform duties not of our choosing, but we're drawn to teaching from a far higher place.

You should name the various commitments you're bringing with you into teaching, spell them out as best you can now so that you have a handy list to post on the bathroom mirror, something to consult each morning as you prepare to dive once more into the everyday contradictions of classroom life and try to live up to the better angels of yourself. Make it simple and true—these are your fundamental commitments to yourself and to your students.

I want to borrow Walt Whitman's opening line as you start to craft your own list: *This is what you shall do.*

Now begin.

⋮ ⋮ ⋮

I'll share a few items from my list here, and maybe some of these points are already on your list, or maybe a couple will resonate with you and find a place there now. But the important thing is to think deeply, reflect fully, and *make your own list.* Do it. Post it. Knowing we will all fall short of our ideals in the rough-and-tumble of real classroom life is no cause for despair or procrastination, and no reason not to posit the ideals you're reaching for— we can try to end each day critical of every failure and shortcoming, and get up next morning ready to go at it again, and this time do it all a bit better.

Here are commitments that I see and affirm each day on my way to my classroom, my concise reminders to myself, a kind of personal looking-glass list:

- Every student who comes through the classroom door is a three-dimensional human being like myself, and a person of infinite and incalculable value, someone to be treated with awe and respect, humility and patience, deep esteem and even reverence.

- Today and every day (and in a zillion ways) we're learning to live together—the environment we strive to create is characterized by honesty, dialogue, self-respect and respect for others, critical questioning, fairness, and recognition, not monologue, management, control, or punishment.
- In everything we undertake we foreground the arts of liberty—imagination and creativity, initiative and courage, compassion, ingenuity, and enterprise—as we work to expand the confidence and agency of students, acknowledge and affirm their intelligence, and generate transformative possibilities for all of us.
- Wherever racism—as well as other forms of group oppression—exists, I will resist.
- I'll practice what I teach: When I say be a good reader, I'll work to be a better reader; when I say be a good citizen or community resident, I'll show them what joining the larger community looks like.
- I'll do my best to be honest and truthful to students (even about the standardized tests—OMG—even about the curriculum and the school structures, even about racism).

That's just a start, and it's already daunting. To make it more so, I want to elaborate on telling the truth—the raw and unvarnished, difficult and often unwelcome, sometimes subversive and risky but also absolutely necessary, truth. Telling the truth is not wielding dogma like a weapon, nor is it living in a relativistic fantasy land. If we don't try to tell the truth we're trapped in a bughouse, and bedlam surrounds us; if we don't tell the truth we can't develop effective strategies for overcoming obstacles and righting wrongs; if we don't tell the truth we can't work toward mutual understanding—so I'll try to tell the truth to my students as I understand it, and we can struggle together toward deeper truths as we move along.

Here's a truth-telling piece to practice, especially for those teaching in urban (and, with some variations, other) schools (this example is directed at preservice teachers): "You've likely come to teaching with hope and the best of intentions, but you should know that the system you'll be joining hates Black and Brown and poor kids—it sounds harsh and unyielding and extreme, but try not to recoil or turn away. I have the factual evidence that the system is organized to miseducate these

> I'll try to tell the truth to my students as I understand it, and we can struggle together toward deeper truths as we move along.

children, and it includes, in Chicago for example, the shameful lack of resources, enforced racial segregation, the dumbed-down and Eurocentric curriculum accompanied by a stifling top-down pedagogy, arcane rules and routines that result predictably in social shaming and widespread exclusions. We're all asked to participate mindlessly in that nasty work without raising our voices in opposition, but I'll try (as we all should try) to build my capacities to tell the truth about that, and to be heard."

The dominant American narrative that glibly labels the Black community as primarily pathological, and Black children and youth as nothing but a collection of pitiable or dangerous deficits, is not true, and I disavow the dismal American habit that blames both poverty and racism on the imagined misbehaviors of poor and Black people. I hope you, like me, want to seek out the generative and ever-hopeful lessons of radical love and expansive empathy, which are relevant whatever your race or ethnicity or background. White people (specifically) can work to become useful allies and effective organizers, although "ally" isn't quite the right word here because it gestures too easily toward charity as an adequate intervention against racism, White or male supremacy, or heteronormativity. It's not. We all need to become agents of change, solidarity, and transformation—not a squad of missionaries on a campaign of uplift—if we're to dismantle the racial hierarchy and create the conditions for everyone to get free—not patronizing sentiments but a commitment to equity, justice, recognition, humanization, and emancipation.

> We all need to become agents of change, solidarity, and transformation—not a squad of missionaries on a campaign of uplift—if we're to dismantle the racial hierarchy and create the conditions for everyone to get free.

:   :   :

Humanization and dehumanization—these quarreling twins define the landscapes of learning, and they make holding onto the living, ethical heart of teaching hard, grinding, often contentious and sometimes courageous work. The twins clash and struggle, become impossibly entangled and difficult to separate. It's not as if two distinct paths are clearly laid out before us—the bright heavenly path set with palm fronds, and the dark devilish path of briars and brambles. It's not as if at the end of the road there are two neat packages to choose from, one decorated with ribbons and roses, the other marked with a skull and crossbones. If it were like this we would live always and forever on the side of the angels. There would be only simple scripts to follow.

But reality isn't like this. The daily choices we make in classrooms are murkier, denser, more layered and more difficult. The implications of our choices aren't always clear, the long-term effects not only unknown to us, but often unknowable as well. We walk our wobbly pathway as best we can, with hope certainly, but without guarantees. All the more reason to hold in our consciousness the dimensions of what is at stake: humanity's capacity, drive, and potential for forward motion, the propulsive possibility of enlightenment, the unending quest for human freedom. All the more reason to bring to the surface our moral commitments for examination and argument. All the more reason—as we make our twisty way—to state from the outset our overriding commitments to our students, and through them to all of humanity.

How odd, then, that this dimension and the fundamental choices involved go so completely unacknowledged and unspoken in our schools, not to mention in the wider world. There is much talk about skills, but nothing about liberation. There are in-school seminars on classroom management and discipline, staff development workshops on lesson planning, but nothing on strategies to teach toward freedom. The linear, the instrumental, the serviceable are emphasized without thought or question. The moral and the ethical are ignored, obscured, and obfuscated, also without much thought.

In colleges of education it's the same story. Professors and graduate students can be rewarded for pursuing programs of research on teaching that are equal parts received thinking, "proven" methods, and borrowed logic, papered over and painted silver to dazzle the credulous with the shine of "real science." And teacher education and credentialing programs also do some bad work when students dabble in educational philosophy, educational psychology, history of education, then dip into a few courses on the methods of teaching, and finally try to bring it all together in a semester of student teaching. This approach structures the separation of thought from action, and nowhere elevates the moral and the ethical to a central place. All of this ignores the humanizing mission of teaching.

I would love to see all teacher preparation and graduate programs offer a course of study centered on the humanistic mission of the enterprise: Turning Toward My Student as a Fellow Creature; Building a Republic of Many Voices and a Community With and For Students; Feeling the Weight of the World Through Your Own Lifting Arms; Teaching Toward Freedom.

> There is no promised land in teaching, just that aching, persistent tension between reality and possibility.

I hope you're aware by now that there is no simple technique or linear path that will take you to where you need to go, and then allow you to live out a settled teaching life, untroubled and finished. There is no promised land in teaching, just that aching, persistent tension between reality and possibility. I hope you become a student of your students, and then create a community through dialogue. I hope you now have in hand that wild and eclectic and dynamic list that you can refer to every day on your way to school, or anytime you're feeling lost or lonely.

I hope you've figured out what you're teaching for, and what you're teaching against. I want to teach against oppression and subjugation, exploitation, unfairness, and unkindness. I want to teach toward freedom, for enlightenment and awareness, wide-awakeness, protection of the weak, cooperation, generosity, compassion, and love. I want my teaching to mean something worthwhile in the lives of my students and in the larger worlds they will inhabit and create. I want it to mean something in mine. I hope you have your own wild and free teaching dreams.

The First Day
of School Has Arrived!

Ready . . . Set . . . TEACH!

4:30 a.m., and you're up before the alarm sounds.

Lunch packed the night before and nestled in the refrigerator, backpack and water bottle ready by the door. Time for an abbreviated morning routine—a quick run or swim or walk in the morning air, perhaps, or some deep breathing and mind-clearing. On to a hot shower, a look in the mirror to consult your list of commitments, a bagel, and a cup of coffee before heading to school. Remember to hydrate!

The classroom is set up, each inch reflecting your best thinking about students and learning, about your passions and priorities, about your teaching values and your largest goals for the year.

You've rehearsed how you'll greet each student, your opening words and first class meeting, how you'll set the right tone and feel as you work into the rhythm of the day.

You'll be there by 7:00, even though the kids won't arrive until 8:30.

They'll be nervous too.

Breathe in, breathe out.

How exciting, this magic moment. Experience it; live it; marinate on it. You're a teacher at last!

About the Author

William Ayers, Distinguished Professor of Education and Senior University Scholar at the University of Illinois at Chicago (retired), has written extensively about social justice and democracy, education and the cultural contexts of schooling, and teaching as an essentially intellectual, ethical, and political enterprise. He edits the Teaching for Social Justice series for Teachers College Press. He published his first book, *The Good Preschool Teacher,* with TCP in 1989, and this is his 12th book with the press. His other books include *Teaching with Conscience in an Imperfect World; A Kind and Just Parent; Teaching Toward Freedom; Fugitive Days; Teaching the Personal and the Political; Public Enemy; Teaching the Taboo* (with Rick Ayers); *On the Side of the Child; A Light in Dark Times; To Teach: The Journey, in Comics* (with Ryan Alexander-Tanner); and *Demand the Impossible!*

He lives in Hyde Park, Chicago, with his partner of 50 years, Bernardine Dohrn.